Crash Course in Cataloging for Non-Catalogers

Recent Titles in
Libraries Unlimited Crash Course Series

Crash Course in Cataloging for Non-Catalogers

A Casual Conversation on Organizing Information

Allison G. Kaplan

Crash Course

A Member of the Greenwood Publishing Group

Westport, Connecticut • London

Library of Congress Cataloging-in-Publication Data

Kaplan, Allison G.

  Crash course in cataloging for non-catalogers : a casual conversation on organizing information / Allison G. Kaplan.

        p. cm. — (Libraries Unlimited crash course series)
  Includes bibliographical references and index.
  ISBN 978–1–59158–401–8 (alk. paper)
  1. Cataloging.   2. Information organization.   I. Title.
Z693.K283   2009
025.3—dc22   2008050216

British Library Cataloguing in Publication Data is available.

Library of Congress Catalog Card Number: 2008050216
ISBN: 978–1–59158–401–8

First published in 2009

Libraries Unlimited, 88 Post Road West, Westport, CT 06881
A Member of the Greenwood Publishing Group, Inc.
www.lu.com

Printed in the United States of America

The paper used in this book complies with the Permanent Paper Standard issued by the National Information Standards Organization (Z39.48–1984).

10 9 8 7 6 5 4 3 2 1

Copyright Acknowledgments

All copyright rights in the Dewey Decimal Classification are owned by OCLC Online Computer Library Center, Inc. The summaries are used with OCLC's permission. *DDC, Dewey* and *Dewey Decimal Classification* are registered trademarks of OCLC Online Computer Library Center, Inc.

Screenshots from OPALS used with permission.

Dedicated to Eric
For his love of spiders and for his patience with my questions;
To David, Rebekah, and Hannah, as always and with love;
and
To you, the reader, for bravely venturing into the world of cataloging.

CONTENTS

ACKNOWLEDGMENTS

When Blanche Woolls first approached me to write this book, I had to give the matter some thought. After much patience on Blanche's part and with many false starts on my part, this book was finally completed on the eve of a cataloging revolution. However, while it is true that the mechanics of cataloging materials may be changing, the theory of organizing collections, especially print-based collections of smaller public and school libraries, will, I believe, remain relatively unchanged. That having been said, please note that the reader will find very little cataloging theory in this book; I've tried to include only as much theory as was necessary to explain the practice. The information here is meant to be presented in a very casual way, as if the reader and I were having our own conversation about cataloging. I hope you, the reader, will find this book helpful and fun to read.

Nothing is ever created in a vacuum. I am indebted to the public library managers and librarians with whom I spoke who provided examples of cataloging problems that exist in the small public library setting. The advice and requests for help from you all has been invaluable, and I hope your ideas and thoughts are accurately presented here. Special thanks go to Mary King, director of the Moore Memorial Library in Greene, New York, for providing sample pages of some local history publications. Thanks also to Pat Shufeldt, conference co-chair for the 2008 national conference of the Church and Synagogue Library Association, for her comments on a draft of this manuscript and help with the OPALS program. I would also like to thank my new colleagues at the University of Wisconsin—Madison, Drs. Michele Besant and Kyung-Sun Kim, whose support and good humor while I was writing this book was and is very much appreciated. And of course to my family, who support me in all of my great adventures.

INTRODUCTION

READY!

Congratulations! You are now working in, or are in charge of, a community library! You are so happy to have this job and to be making such an important contribution to your community. But you are also worried. You have not had very much training as a librarian, you do not have a library science degree, and you are concerned that you will not be successful at your job. Being the director of, or simply working in, a small library without any formal training can indeed be a daunting task.

You may be thinking that you don't need to know anything about cataloging because you buy all of your items already cataloged or you are part of a library system or group that takes care of cataloging your items. This is not true. Even if you never have to catalog an item, if you never have to change a subject heading, if you never have to tape a classification number to a book, you need to know something about cataloging. You need to understand why the library is organized the way it is, because some day you will have to tell a library user why folklore books are shelved in the non-fiction section; or you will have to add a subject heading to an item because the subject headings provided by the system cataloger are just not detailed enough for your users; or you will need to help someone figure out why some books about World War II are classified under 940.53 and others are classified with the history of a specific country.

As part of the *Crash Course* series, it is not the objective of this small book to make you a professional cataloger. Nor it is the intent of the author to suggest that one should run a library without a formal education in library science. However, we know that people do run libraries without a lot of formal education, and so it is the objective of this book to help you make informed decisions about the organization of your library.

Running a small, rural library means that you are part of a community that may be miles away from a major metropolitan area and an institute of higher education. But it does not necessarily mean that you are disconnected from the world around you. Besides reading this book and working through the problem sets, we highly recommend that you contact the nearest library and information science program near you and find out about distance education opportunities available to you. The web site for the American Library Association education page (http://www.ala.org/ala/educationcareers/index.cfm) can also be a useful place for you to get information about taking classes.

SET!

Many people find the thought of cataloging library materials pretty scary. Lots of library school graduates have told me that the only time they cried in library school was when they took the cataloging class! Indeed, cataloging class in formal library programs may well be the class that students are least likely to be excited about taking. Having said that, the information and training provided in that class is essential to the management of a library regardless of the size or format of that library, so taking cataloging should form a core of library education.

But we're not here to scare you, and you are not reading this book because you want to be scared. You need some information about how to organize your library collection. Therefore, the information presented here will be presented in an open and non-threatening way with the hope that you will be eager to read more about, or even take a class in, cataloging and classification.

This book focuses on the basics of organizing library collections. There is no assumption that you have had any previous experience or training in this area. It is meant to provide information in a relaxed manner and to ease you into wanting to know more about library organization and cataloging. The use of technical library words has been kept to a minimum as much as possible. However, there are cases in which there is no substitute for the technical term. In this case, a definition is provided in the text as well as in the glossary section of the book.

Cataloging is the term used to discuss how library items are organized in the library. These items may be books, DVDs, or magazines that have physical locations on shelves. These items may also include "virtual" items, or information that is electronic in format such as a web site, digitized photograph, or an electronic book. Regardless of the physical properties of the items, they have to be organized in a way that makes it easy for the people in your library to find and use them. Although there are lots of cataloging rules, you don't have to memorize them all to manage your collection. However, you do need to be familiar enough with the rules to know when you can or cannot change the organization of the item. That's why this book was written: to help you become a good consumer of cataloging.

In this book there are several references to Internet resources and screen shots. All sources (URLs) and search results are accurate as of December 1, 2008. Please be aware that because the Internet is a dynamic system it may be that, in following along with the examples, you will get slightly different results from those presented here in this book.

GO!

You are reading this book because you need to know something about organizing library books. You know you should take a class, but for now you need something to get you going. So without further delay, let's find out about cataloging your library materials!

CHAPTER 1

What You Need to Know about Classification

We begin with classification, because it is the part of cataloging that you are most likely to need to change on your own. If we agree that most of us purchase cataloging with our new materials and we agree that most of the time we just file the cards or load the data into our computers, then we will also agree that it's when we put the items on the shelves that we say, "Hmm, wonder how this item ended up here and not over there." Ending up "here" and not "there" is the result of classification. More often than not, it is at the point of shelving materials that we decide if the items have been classified in a way the helps our users find what they are looking for. And so we begin with the aspect of cataloging that is most likely to stop us in our tracks.

There is a great children's book by Jon Scieszka and Lane Smith called *Math Curse*. In this book, the hero comes home from school on Monday with a problem. His math teacher, Mrs. Fibonacci, has told the class, "You know, you can think of almost everything as a math problem."[1] Our poor hero then spends the next day seeing all of his activities as math problems. From English to Social Studies to Physical Education, even to the amount of milk he pours into his morning cereal; everything is put into a math problem and it is driving our hero nuts. Finally he figures out how to deal with the whole world as a math problem and feels much better, until Wednesday comes along and his science teacher, Mr. Newton, says, "You know, you can think of almost everything as a science experiment!"[2]

Not that I want to upset you or anything, but you know, you *can* think of almost everything as a classification problem! Honest! Take your local supermarket or grocery store as an example. Look around and think about what you see. Do you see carrots next to cereal? Do you see shampoo next to cheese? No, of course not! What you do see is all of the fruits and vegetables together; all of the shampoos and soaps together; and all of the milk products together. These things are arranged according to some plan by the owner of the store. The owner has noticed how shoppers look for things and arranges the items in the store accordingly. The owner has "classified" the items in the store. You, the shopper, have come to accept this classification system. Over time you learn how things were arranged; maybe you even ask for help in finding certain items until the time comes when you know exactly where to go for your carrots, cereal, shampoo, and cheese.

Now think of what happens when you go to a store someplace else and you discover that the way that store is arranged is different from how you are used to a grocery store being organized. Think of how irritated you get when you think you are going in the right direction to get your shampoo and it turns out that the owner of this store has put the shampoo someplace else. When that happens to me, I think to myself, "Just how *does* this place organize its stuff!?" Think too about how frustrating it can be to find something that doesn't quite fit the classification scheme of the store. I know I always have a hard time finding glue. Is it classified with the hardware stuff or the school supplies stuff? Sometimes it's in both places, and sometimes it's someplace else altogether. What a hassle!

To have some kind of order to a group of objects, it has to be "classified." What is classification? **Classification** is the organization of items according to specific groups. We classify objects in our lives every day. For example, take a look at this list of items:

Televisions   DVD players   Radios   MP3 players

How can we classify these items? Well, we might put them all together in one big category because they are all entertainment devices. Just a few items are here, so arranging them in one pile might be all right. But what happens if in a few years there are even more entertainment machines? Then we end up with a big messy pile of stuff. What else could we do?

We might put televisions and DVD players in one group because they show moving pictures and play sound together and put radios in another group because they are used only for sound. But what do we do with MP3 players that can be used in three ways; to play just sound, to play both sound and pictures, or to just display pictures? Perhaps MP3 players are in a class by themselves? But what would happen if we put the MP3 players in their own category and in a few years there are lots of different types of entertainment machines that are also unique and might also be in categories of their own? In this case we have too many small piles; just the opposite problem of our big entertainment pile. If a "class" is a single group of like items, in our case the televisions and the DVD players, then "classification" is the act of putting like items into groups. But how do we know what those groups are? If we have a pile of televisions and DVD players on one table and radios in a pile on another table, how would we know what the groupings, or classifications, are? We could put a sign on each table like this: *"Things that play back pictures and sound together"* and *"Things that play back only sound."* Those would have to be big signs! To make the signs smaller, we could abbreviate them to something like this: "PPS" (meaning play back pictures and sound) and "PSO" (meaning play back sound only). That's much more manageable, but we have to teach people the meaning of PPS and PSO, which might take some doing.

In the library world, we think of classification as using numbers, letters, or a mix of numbers and letters as a kind of shorthand or abbreviation to note how similar materials are grouped together. If you walk around your library, you might see something like "636.1," "636.8," or "FIC" on your items. This is a short way of saying, "The items here are about horses," for 636.1; "The items here are about cats," for 636.8; and, "The items here are fiction," for FIC. We see that using the shorthand is much more practical than writing out big signs. Classification helps us keep our books about horses in one place, our books about cats in another, and our fiction books in another. The standard rules help to make sure that the organization in one library is very similar to the organization in another library. We use the short signs and have to teach people what 636.1, 636.8, and FIC mean, but for the most part this standard way of classification seems to work pretty well.

In the next section we are going to learn about the art of classification. But the art of classification is truly an art form. Even with all of the rules we have, there are lots of instances (just like our case of classifying glue in our grocery stores) where we have to make some tough choices.

THE DEWEY DECIMAL CLASSIFICATION SYSTEM

A great story it is told about Melvil Dewey, the creator of the Dewey Decimal Classification system, and how he "discovered" his classification system. For many years, great library thinkers had been wondering about the best ways of keeping library materials organized, Dewey included. Dewey recalls that one day he was sitting in church and the idea just came to him. He relates how he was so excited that he nearly jumped out of his seat and yelled, "Eureka!" We don't know if this is a completely true account of how he did it, but we do know that many of our public and school libraries are organized using ten main classes or groups of knowledge, known today as the **Dewey Decimal Classification** (DDC) system, and that Mr. Dewey is responsible for these classes. In Figure 1.1 we can see what those ten main classes are.

Much can be discussed about these ten main classes. The first thing to discuss is the list itself. Melvil Dewey created this list in 1876, more than 100 years ago. So

000   Computer science, information & general works

100   Philosophy & psychology

200   Religion

300   Social sciences

400   Language

500   Science

600   Technology

700   Arts & recreation

800   Literature

900   History & geography

Figure 1.1.   List of the ten main classes of the Dewey Decimal Classification system.
Reprinted with permission from OCLC © 2004.

many things were different in those days. While the basic structure of the classes is similar to the original, the types of things published today are so vastly different from the 1800s. Notice for example the very first classification category, "000 Computer science, information & general works." Mr. Dewey was very smart, but there is no way he could have foreseen the place computers would have in our twenty-first-century lives. In fact, Mr. Dewey did not have a "000" classification in the first edition of his work in 1876. It was not until the second edition in 1885 that "0" first appeared and was used for "General Works." As we further explore this classification scheme, we will have to be patient with Mr. Dewey and the century he lived in. Many early versions of Mr. Dewey's works are available online from Google Books. Just for fun, go to Google Books at http://books.google.com and type in the search "dewey classification" (without the quotation marks) to see the copies of Mr. Dewey's works.

When Dewey published his classification system in 1876 it was 44 pages. Today, the DDC is published in four volumes. Many large public libraries use the full four-volume set when cataloging their items; however, the four-volume set is not cheap. It provides directions for very detailed classification, but it requires a great deal of cataloging knowledge to use properly. Most school and smaller public libraries rely on the abridged version of DDC for cataloging purposes. The abridged version comes in one volume, it is much less expensive to buy, and it can be used without a tremendous amount of previous cataloging training. The drawback is that one cannot catalog with as much detail as with the four-volume set. However, in dealing with smaller collections (recommendation of 20,000 volumes or less) not as much detail is required anyway. Therefore, when we talk about DDC in this book, we are referring to the abridged version; specifically, the 14th edition of the abridged version that was published in 2004.

After Mr. Dewey jumped up and nearly yelled, "Eureka," things really got interesting. The American Library Association had been recently created, and the leaders were all excited about Dewey's classification and other innovations in the profession. The classification system and the organization of information on cards for card catalogs became standardized, and now a patron could walk into any library and feel comfortable looking for specific subjects much as we feel comfortable going into any store knowing that all the milk products will be located together in one place. While the rules for creating a catalog record were still being standardized, the Dewey Decimal Classification system had quickly become the way to organizes books on the shelves.

KEEPING DDC CURRENT

The 14th edition of the abridged DDC includes a lot of information besides the numbers themselves. Information is there about the history of the system, changes between the previous edition and the current one, a glossary of classification terms, and directions on how to use the abridged system. The abridged edition is updated roughly every seven years. The 14th edition was published in 2004, so we can expect a new edition to be published around 2011. Each new edition of both the abridged and unabridged volumes has taken into account changes in the type of information being published, changes in society, and changes in technology. Updating the classifications is crucial for keeping current with society. Recalling that the system was first published in 1876 and thinking about how we view such topics as women, religion, work, and even fiction and how differently those topics were treated over 100 years ago, we can see how important it is to constantly revise the numbers. However, revising the numbers isn't without problems. Each time a number changes librarians have to decide what they are going to do with the items already classified under the old numbers. Shifting numbers, such as moving "word processing" from 652.5 to 005.52, can be problematic depending on how many items have to be relabeled and moved around. Furthermore, introducing a new number, such as 006.8 for "virtual reality," can also cause some problems. It comes down to deciding if there is time and money to shift things around or if the library users are going to have to learn to look in two places for the same topic. Despite some of the drawbacks to changing numbers, the classification needs to be revised to keep up with a changing society.

The 14th edition book has a companion in the online environment under the title of Abridged Web Dewey. The advantage of purchasing a site license for access to Abridged Web Dewey is that it links the DDC number to the right Library of Congress or *Sears* subject headings. This is a very nice feature, although the Library of Congress subject headings are available for free from the Library of Congress web site. More discussion about subject headings will be found in chapter 2. The other advantage of Abridged Web Dewey is that changes to DDC made on a quarterly basis are incorporated into the web site, making it easy to follow the updates, whereas the book format

000 Computer science, knowledge & systems	*500 Science*
010 Bibliographies	510 Mathematics
020 Library & information sciences	520 Astronomy
030 Encyclopedias & books of facts	530 Physics
040 [Unassigned]	540 Chemistry
050 Magazines, journals & serials	550 Earth sciences & geology
060 Associations, organizations & museums	560 Fossils & prehistoric life
070 News media, journalism & publishing	570 Life sciences; biology
080 Quotations	580 Plants (Botany)
090 Manuscripts & rare books	590 Animals (Zoology)
100 Philosophy	*600 Technology*
110 Metaphysics	610 Medicine & health
120 Epistemology	620 Engineering
130 Parapsychology & occultism	630 Agriculture
140 Philosophical schools of thought	640 Home & family management
150 Psychology	650 Management & public relations
160 Logic	660 Chemical engineering
170 Ethics	670 Manufacturing
180 Ancient, medieval & eastern philosophy	680 Manufacture for specific uses
190 Modern western philosophy	690 Building & construction
200 Religion	*700 Arts*
210 Philosophy & theory of religion	710 Landscaping & area planning
220 The Bible	720 Architecture
230 Christianity & Christian theology	730 Sculpture, ceramics & metalwork
240 Christian practice & observance	740 Drawing & decorative arts
250 Christian pastoral practice & religious orders	750 Painting
260 Christian organization, social work & worship	760 Graphic arts
270 History of Christianity	770 Photography & computer art
280 Christian denominations	780 Music
290 Other religions	790 Sports, games & entertainment
300 Social sciences, sociology & anthropology	*800 Literature, rhetoric & criticism*
310 Statistics	810 American literature in English
320 Political science	820 English & Old English literatures
330 Economics	830 German & related literatures
340 Law	840 French & related literatures
350 Public administration & military science	850 Italian, Romanian & related literatures
360 Social problems & social services	860 Spanish & Portuguese literatures
370 Education	870 Latin & Italic literatures
380 Commerce, communications & transportation	880 Classical & modern Greek literatures
390 Customs, etiquette & folklore	890 Other literatures
400 Language	*900 History*
410 Linguistics	910 Geography & travel
420 English & Old English languages	920 Biography & genealogy
430 German & related languages	930 History of ancient world (to ca. 499)
440 French & related languages	940 History of Europe
450 Italian, Romanian & related languages	950 History of Asia
460 Spanish & Portuguese languages	960 History of Africa
470 Latin & Italic languages	970 History of North America
480 Classical & modern Greek languages	980 History of South America
490 Other languages	990 History of other areas

Figure 1.2.   The Second Summary: The Hundred Divisions. (Emphasis added.)
Reprinted with permission © OCLC, 2004.

is updated only every seven years. However, when you buy the book you can also purchase the paper version of the quarterly updates so you can still keep current even if you are using the book.

USING DDC

This section will present information about the organization of the DDC system. It cannot provide step-by-step instructions for how to use DDC because to do so would require having the DDC book in hand and providing detail that is the beyond the purpose of this book. However, if you do have the 14th edition of the abridged DDC, now would be a good time to bring it out. If you don't, this discussion will be general enough to understand how DDC is structured. What this section will not do is enable you to classify your collection without having DDC in your hands.

DDC is broken into several parts, the largest of which is referred to as "Tables." The tables include standard subdivisions, the three "Summaries," and the "Schedules." We will tackle the standard subdivisions and schedules later in this section. Right now we want to look at the Summaries. The **summaries** take us through the expansion of the classes from the ten main classes to the hundred divisions to the thousand sections. Let's look again at the main classes in Figure 1.1 as shown on page 4.

Let's think of these classes as places in general at the store. From the ten main classes we have a general idea of where things might be located but not a complete picture. In our store we have a general idea of where the refrigerated items are, but we don't know what exactly we will find in that section. In the library, the ten main classes may tell us where we might find a book about animals, but we do not have a very good sense of where we might find a book about a specific animal. The store puts up signs to help us with the details. Likewise, Dewey provided us with "divisions" to help us get a better idea of what's in the "classes." The next summary is called "The Hundred Divisions" (see Figure 1.2).

In this figure we see that the lines in italics (000, 100, 200, 300, and so on) match the names of our main 10 classes. The information within each class (lines 010, 020, etc.) give us that small amount of detail we were looking for. Now we know exactly where we will find our animal books . . . under the number 590. But wait. Although animals are located under number 590, we still might not be sure about our search for a book about cats. A book about the muscles of a cat may well be in 590 for zoology, but what about a book telling us how to take care of our pet cat? Would that book be classed under the 590 number? Not likely. Where might that book be located?

At this point it is not clear where a book about caring for a pet cat might be classified. If we go back to our store, we might see a big sign that says "Dairy" on the wall. We think about all of the things that can be classified as "dairy": milk, cheese, yogurt, and ice cream, to name a few. But we might not be sure about where to find ice cream. Although it is made from cream, which makes it a dairy product, ice cream might be located somewhere other than where you'd expect it to be. Why is this? It is because ice cream is a special kind of dairy product that needs to be kept frozen. Ice cream is in the freezer section of the store. Likewise, a book about caring for pet cats describes more than just the animal itself but how to care for it. Dewey knew this and provided us with a third summary table called "The Thousand Sections" to give us even more detail in the number system. Let's see what the Thousand Sections looks like for zoology and agriculture as shown in Figure 1.3.

Using the Thousand Sections is like walking down the aisle of the grocery store. Now we can see the details of what the store has for sale. Similarly, if we walked down the aisles of the library, we would also see the details of what the library has in each classification. Where will we find our book about cats as pets? Well, maybe it is not crystal clear yet, because we still do not see a number that looks like it would refer to pets. DDC has an index to help us assign a classification number. If you have a copy of DDC abridged, take a look at the index and see if you can find a number for "cats." In the index, we see three references to cats: Cats—636.8; Cats, animal husbandry—636.8; and Cats, zoology—599.75 (p. 850). These numbers bring us to the decimal part of the Dewey Decimal Classification. Let's take a look at that number: 636.8. Looking at Figure 1.3 we see that 636 refers to "Animal Husbandry." In creating his classification system, Dewey used numbers to represent fields of study or disciplines. A person who was interested in raising animals would be interested in animal husbandry. A person interested in the care and feeding of cats would also be interested in animal husbandry. But let's be serious here. How many of our patrons come into our libraries and ask for books on animal husbandry when they are really looking for books about cats as pets?

In the **schedules** part of DDC, numbers are broken down into greater and greater detail. Figure 1.4 shows what the schedule numbers are for the section 636. Now we can see that if we have a book about cats we would have the number 636.8, and if we have a book about dogs we would have the number 636.7. But this information tells us even more about this 636 number. It gives us directions on how to use this number, and it even tells us which other numbers would be better to use depending on the area of study.

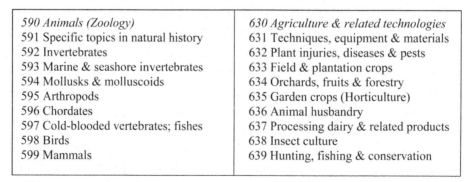

590 Animals (Zoology)	630 Agriculture & related technologies
591 Specific topics in natural history	631 Techniques, equipment & materials
592 Invertebrates	632 Plant injuries, diseases & pests
593 Marine & seashore invertebrates	633 Field & plantation crops
594 Mollusks & molluscoids	634 Orchards, fruits & forestry
595 Arthropods	635 Garden crops (Horticulture)
596 Chordates	636 Animal husbandry
597 Cold-blooded vertebrates; fishes	637 Processing dairy & related products
598 Birds	638 Insect culture
599 Mammals	639 Hunting, fishing & conservation

Figure 1.3.   The Third Summary: The Thousand Sections (partial). (Emphasis added.)
Reprinted with permission © OCLC, 2004.

Two parts of the DDC that we have not yet discussed are referred to in this example. First, look at the note in Figure 1.4: "*See Manual at 800 vs. 398.24, 590, 636.*" The **manual** part of DDC is a helpful guide that helps us decide which number to use if we are unsure. This note tells us to find this place in the manual and see what it says about the relationship between 636 and the other numbers: 800 (literature), 398.24 (tales and folklore of plants and animals), and 590 (animals zoology). If we were to look at those instructions (see p. 101), we would find instructions that if the item is a story (such as *The Black Cat* by Edgar Allen Poe) then classify the book under the number for literature: 800. If the item is a folktale about a cat (such as *Puss in Boots*) then classify

636   Animal husbandry

Including farms, ranches, young of animals

Class here interdisciplinary works on species of domestic animals

Class farms and ranches for, young of specific kinds of animals in 636.1-636.9

For culture of nondomesticated animals, see 639. For a specific

nonagricultural aspect of domestic mammals see the aspect, e.g. biology

of domestic mammals 599.

See Manual at 800 vs. 398.24, 590, 636

Summary

636.001-.009 Standard subdivisions

.08   Specific topics in animal husbandry

.1   Equines   Horses

.2   Ruminants and camel family   Bovines   Cattle

.3   Smaller ruminants   Sheep

.4   Swine

.5   Poultry   Chickens

.6   Birds other than poultry

.7   Dogs

.8   Cats

.9   Other Mammals

Figure 1.4.   The schedule and summary for the DDC number 636.
Reprinted with permission; © OCLC, 2004.

the book under the number for folk tales about animals: 398.24. If the item is about the biological study of cats (such as *Cat Dissection: A Laboratory Guide* by Connie Allen and Valerie Harper) then classify the book under the number for zoology: 590. However, if the book is truly about having a cat as a pet, or breeding cats, or the care and feeding of cats (such as *My First Cat* by Linda Bozzo) then we will use the 636.8 number. The manual is filled with helpful hints to help make classification decisions. If you have the book, it is well worth the time to thumb through that section.

The information in Figure 1.4 also makes mention of the **standard subdivisions**. The standard subdivisions are part of the four tables of information that help identify the following:

- *Table 1:* Format (magazine, encyclopedia, dictionary, etc.) and focus (historical, cultural, or geographic in nature);
- *Table 2:* Geographic or people designation (focus of the item as per a specific location such Wisconsin or Africa, or per a specific group of people such as children or women) in Table 2;
- *Table 3:* Types of literary forms (poetry, drama, etc); and
- *Table 4:* Information about languages (grammar texts, etymology, etc.).

With the exception of Table 1, you must be instructed to use the **tables** to add those numbers to your classification. Unfortunately, there is too much information to reprint the tables here. If you have a copy of DDC, the tables are presented just before the schedules (pages 117–176 in the 14th abridged edition). Numbers from the tables help to make the classification more specific but are not required in creating classification numbers if the collection is small enough so that this kind of detail is not needed. Nevertheless, Table 1 is used so often that it is helpful to have some idea of how it works.

Table 1 is called "Standard Subdivisions." The numbers here can be applied to any classification number unless you are instructed not to add a standard subdivision. This makes Table 1 unique, because all other tables are used only if specifically directed to do so. The standard subdivisions describe the type or focus of the item. If the item is an encyclopedia there is a number to define that. If the item treats a general topic in terms of a specific time period or location, there are numbers for that as well. The main point is that none of the numbers in any of the tables are used by themselves; they will always follow the main class, division, and section numbers.

If this were a cataloging class, I would go into much more detail about how and when to use the tables. The important thing to know about this section is to have the ability to recognize which part of the number has come from the tables so that if you need to shorten a number you will know where it makes the most sense to make the cut. OCLC provides a description of how to use the tables on its web site: http://www.oclc.org/dewey/versions/ddc22print/intro.pdf. It is important to note, however, that the reference is to the full edition of DDC and not the abridged edition. Therefore while reading through this information may be helpful on a theoretical basis, it is not completely helpful for practice. The next section will explore how the numbers are constructed.

CRUNCHING NUMBERS

An excellent workbook for the 13th abridged Dewey is written by Sydney Davis and Gregory New (see Resources list). This book goes into great detail on how to construct classification numbers. Unfortunately, the book has not been revised for the 14th edition, but it is still a useful resource. Given that an entire book has been written on how to create DDC numbers, we cannot hope to cover that material in one small section of this book. However, what you can get here are the tools you need to recognize the structure of the numbers so that you know how much modification you can make to suit your library users.

These days most of us buy materials for our library collections already cataloged. This is helpful to us, but even with professionals doing our cataloging for us we sometimes find the need to make changes. When you purchase cataloging for your materials, find out which edition of DDC is being used to assign the numbers. Is the vendor using the abridged or unabridged version of DDC? Which edition of DDC is being used? It's all right to ask these questions and then make a note of it in your own records. If you have a small collection, you are probably not interested in classification numbers that show the minute detail of the content of the item that is provided in the unabridged DDC. Cookbooks are good examples of numbers that can be long or short. If you have a really big collection of cookbooks, you might want enough detail to keep certain books, such as recipes from India, Greece, and Mexico, all in their separate groups. On the other hand, if you have just a few cookbooks, then separating them out is probably not a big deal. Let's look at the following numbers and see how they are constructed and where we can shorten them.

641.5'9'54   641.5/9/495   641.5 9 72

The first thing we notice is the markings of the apostrophe ('), the slash (/), and the space ( ). These are the typical ways you will see the division of any DDC number they will tell us where we can cut down the number if we need to do so. The second thing we notice is the common part of each of the three numbers—641.59. This number comes from the schedules (see pp. 631–633). We already know from Figure 1.2 that 640 is the number for "Home and family management." If we had the DDC in front of us, we would see that the number 641 is for Food and drink as it relates to household events. The ".5" means Cooking, and ".59" means cooking from specific locations. We can guess then that the remaining numbers, 54, 495, and 72 are the locations for India, Greece, and Mexico. Where did those numbers come from? On page 633, we are informed that if we want to make specific geographic designations we can do so by adding to our base number (641.59) the numbers from Table 2 to show the specific geographic focus of our cookbooks. If we have a large collection of cookbooks then we will want to keep the full numbers. But if we have a small collection we can do one of three things; we can shorten the number all the way to the section number 641 ("Food and drink"); we can shorten the number to the section number plus the subdivision number

641.5 (Cooking in general); or we can shorten the number to the section number plus the two subdivision numbers 641.59 (Cooking from a geographic location). If you go all the way to before the decimal point (641) then all of your items about cooking and drinking in the home will be in one area. In a sense, thinking back to our grocery store, it would be like having all of the canned products lumped together in no particular order just because they are products in cans. If we extend that number just one decimal place (641.5) then we have separated all of the cookbooks from other food and drink type of books. This is sort of like taking the canned vegetables out of that entire pile of other canned goods. Now let's go two decimal places (641.59) and separate the cookbooks from specific countries from the general cookbooks as if we have taken the canned peas and separated them from all of the other canned vegetables. Before we leave our cookbooks, let's take a quick look as the designations for India (54), Greece (495), and Mexico (72). Notice that Greece is given three numbers instead of two. These numbers came from Table 2, which has the whole world divided into 10 sections (after all, this is a decimal system, so everything is divided into 10 parts). Three of these sections have to do with geography in general and seven parts are specific geography: the ancient world, Europe (Western Europe), Asia, Africa, North America, South America, and "other parts of the world and extraterrestrial worlds." India and Mexico are higher up in the divisions for their geographic locations than is Greece. This is not to say that Greece is less important than India or Mexico, only that this is the structure of the table. That is why Greece has three digits and India and Mexico only two. It is possible that you could store your Greek cookbook under the number 641.5949 for cooking from other parts of Western Europe, but then your Greek cookbook would be shelved together with those from Iceland, Belgium, Switzerland, Serbia, and other unrelated areas. For my money, it is worth going the extra digit and keeping the Greek cookbook with other Greek cookbooks. But that judgment is all part of the art of cataloging!

Let's take another set of numbers and see if we can figure out the pattern. Our items cover the history of World War II in general as well as from the German perspective, the Russian perspective, and the American perspective. Here are our numbers:

940.53   943.086   947.084   973.917

With the exception of one number—973.917—the common element is 94-. Looking back at Figure 1.2, we know that the 900s are the class for history and that 940 is history of Western Europe and 970 is history of North America. We also notice that there are no markings to tell us where to cut short the numbers. World War II is of special historical significance for the entire world. Therefore, it has its own number designation: 940.53. One cannot make that number any shorter. A note under the number 940.53 states if the item is about the military participation in the war then class it under 940.53, but if the item is about the effects of the war on that country then classify it under the country. Our numbers (943.086, 947.084, 973.917) tell us that these items are about the effects of the war in a particular country and not about military participation. This is another example of how the notes in the schedules are helpful in guiding us to making the right decision.

Now that we're all right with those other numbers, let's take them apart. The classification number 943.086 is used for the history of Germany from 1933–1945 (p. 784). That certainly covers the World War II time period. The same is seen for 947.084 (history of Russia 1917–1991) and for 973.917 (history of the United States 1933–1945). Notice that the Russian historical time period is broader than the actual years of World War II. We are not allowed to make up our own time periods. We use the 1917–1991 time period because that is what DDC has given us and because the World War II time period fits within those dates.

Cutter Numbers

Notice that the classification number is used to show the discipline the item covers but that all items in the same discipline could have the same classification number. For example, if we had 10 books about World War II, they would all have the same classification number: 940.53. We add to the classification number to make what is often referred to as a **call number** that shows the author or date of publication. The part of the number that is not the classification part is often called the "cutter," which brings us to another giant in the library profession: Charles A. Cutter.

Mr. Cutter was a pioneer in the field of cataloging around the same time as Mr. Dewey. Cutter devised a set of rules for cataloging that we will explore in chapter 3. He also devised a way to make each book number unique by adding to the classification number an alphanumeric designation for the author or title of the book. This combination of letters and numbers to represent the author of the book became very popular, and Mr. Cutter is rewarded for all time with having us refer to this alphanumeric number as a cutter number. Creating a cutter number is called "cuttering."

Cuttering involves using something called "Cutter Tables" and finding the number that matches the author's last name (or first word of the title of the item if there is no author; see chapter 3). Then the chart will provide a number to go with the name. Years ago we had long, hard cardboard books with rows and rows of numbers. Today we have a free online program provided by OCLC that automatically generates the number for you. This is a great boon to the in-house cataloger. The resource is called the "Dewey Cutter Program" and is available at http://www.oclc.org/dewey/support/program/default.htm. The program offers the choice of the Cutter-Sanborn Four-Figure Table or the Cutter Four-Figure Table. To figure out which table is best for you, take a look at the collection you already have. If you see something like An2455, then you want to use the Cutter Four-Figure Table. If you see A245 then you will select the Cutter-Sanborn Four-Figure Table.

Here's how the classification and cutter numbers work together. Let's go back to our general World War II books. Let's say that we have four books; three by Kaplan and one by Kapolei. Of the three Kaplan books, one is titled *The Eight Causes of World War II* and was published in 1998; the two other are both titled *How the War Was Won*, but one was published in 1998 and the other in 2006. Since they all cover the same discipline, we know that the number will be 940.53. Now let's see how the cutter numbers give each book an individual identity. Figure 1.5 shows the call numbers for each of the four books; Kaplan's *Eight Causes of World War II*, Kaplan's *How the War Was Won* with the 1998 publication data, Kaplan's *How the War Was Won* with the 2006 publication date, and Kapolei's book respectively.

We can see in Figure 1.5 some differences in the numbers. First let's establish that we used the OCLC program for getting cutter numbers. This accounts for the "K172" and "K176" that we see in the figure. Now let's examine each number. Our first number, "940.53 K172e 1998," puzzles us just a little because of that "e" at the end of the cutter number. Kaplan wrote two books about the same topic that were published in the same year. In order for us to know the difference between the two, we use what is called a "work mark" for one of the titles. A **work mark** is usually the first letter of the first word of the title added to the cutter number to differentiate two publications by the same author in the same year so that the call number is unique for each publication. In our example the title is *The Eight Causes of World War II*. Notice that we skipped the initial article "The" because cataloging rules tell us to do that. Skipping the initial article will come up again in chapter 4, so it's a good idea to remember that in cataloging we tend to ignore the initial articles (a, an, the) of a title of a work.

Our next two numbers are exactly the same except for the date. With these two numbers we show that the items are the same but were published in two different years. Our last number does not have a publication date. Most libraries automatically include the publication date in the call number, but we don't have that information and so we've left that part out.

If all of this business of creating a cutter number is confusing you, then join the club. Many school and small public libraries are now adopting the practice of simply using the first three letters of the author's last name instead of a cutter number. In our examples we would then have the information as presented in Figure 1.6.

While this is certainly easier to do, it can create two problems. First, it does not help us to know the different between Kaplan's works and Kapolie's works. It forces the users to take extra care in making sure they have picked up the right work. Second, if the library already has some works with the cutter numbers and then switches to the author names, how should the works be filed on the shelf? Do we put all of the works with the cutter numbers after the works with just the letters? Or, do we try to interfile the items hoping that somehow the users will understand what we are trying to do? Or do we spend the time and huge expense to relabel all of our items and fix the classification numbers in our database? It is a sticky problem for which there is no final answer. As the cataloger for your library, you will need to make a decision and stick to it as much as possible.

940.53 K172e 1998	940.53 K172 1998	940.53 K172 2006	940.53 K176

Figure 1.5.   Call number examples.

940.53	940.53	940.53	940.53
KAPe	KAP	KAP	KAP
1998	1998	2006	

Figure 1.6.   Classification examples using author names instead of cutter numbers.

A WORD OF CAUTION ABOUT CLASSIFICATION

Several areas cause problems for the new cataloger when assigning classification numbers: works of fiction, biographies, and magazines. None of these types of items were collected in any serious manner when Dewey was creating his classification system, and so he pretty much ignored them. However, as public libraries and school libraries started using the system, they found that they had to find ways of dealing with the materials that mattered most to their users.

Fiction

Dewey created a classification system that addresses most needs for non-fiction works. We have not looked at an area that comprises a huge portion of our library collections—fiction. Keep a few things in mind when using Dewey for fiction collections. First, in 1876 there were great works of literature and rhetoric, and there was the dime novel. A library collection included great works of literature: those of Shakespeare, Dickens, Keats, and Chaucer. Western fiction, mysteries, romance novels, and the like were simply not part of the library collection. Second, children's literature was just starting to make its way into the publishing industry beyond works for educational purposes. Collections of folk tales for the sake of entertainment were virtually unheard of. No Caldecott, Newberry, Coretta Scott King, or Printz award–winning books existed. All of these types of publications now take up a huge part of our library collections. While we still also collect "classic" literature, the line between classic and pure fiction becomes more and more blurry. Dewey did not anticipate the growth of the fiction collection, and so we don't really have a standard way of dealing with it.

Technically speaking, all fiction works could be classified under the Literature class or 800 number. However, most of us have a separate fiction collection using the classification designation of "FIC." This certainly seems to serve the purpose for organizing our fiction collections. Companies who sell library materials also offer stickers for the spines of the books with pictures of cowboys, hearts, and magnifying glasses to help illustrate the genre of fiction for each item. Some libraries will actually have their fiction collections organized by genre type (for example, Westerns, mysteries, and romance), but others have small enough collections where a mixture of "FIC" and stickers is satisfactory.

Children's literature is a completely different situation. We teach our children patrons that if the call number begins with a number such as 016 or 636, then it is a work of non-fiction; it is a true story. We still have to explain the 800 section to them and what makes something a "classic" piece of literature. However, our biggest problem is the number 398.2 and all of its subdivisions. The number 398.2 is for folk literature. Certainly, our young users would argue, folk tales are not true stories. And they would be right. To understand why folk tales are classified under a non-fiction number, we have to understand a little bit of the history of the publication of folk tales.

Most of us are familiar with Little Red Riding Hood, Hansel and Gretel, and many other folk tales. What you might not know is that folk tales were used originally to teach, not to entertain. Or that our favorite "authors" of folk tales, the Brothers Grimm, did not go around the German countryside in the late 1700s and early 1800s to collect fun stories for kids but to collect folk tales to study and analyze. Knowing these two facts we can now explain why the Grimm and other folk tales are classified along with non-fiction works.

The 398.2 classification works just fine for "real" folk tales, but we get into trouble when contemporary authors mess around with the folk tales. Instances like James Marshall's *Little Red Riding Hood,* Robin Mckinley's *Beauty,* William Wegman's *Cinderella,* or Donna Jo Napoli's *Zel* are stories that are all adaptations of classic folk tales but are so far removed from the tales that they are considered fiction and classified as such. The author we have to be careful of is Hans Christian Andersen. One definition of folk tales is that there is no author. The Brothers Grimm are often assigned "authorship" of certain folk tales, but the truth is that they were really only editors. They went through the countryside collecting the stories, but they did not make up the stories themselves. Not so with Mr. Andersen. Andersen wrote his own stories, even if he took themes from folk tales that he had grown up with. *The Little Mermaid, The Steadfast Soldier,* and the others are all his stories, and so, like the *Steadfast Soldier,* stand firmly in the area of fiction. Because his stories have taken on the characteristics of folk tales, it is not uncommon to see Andersen stories in the folk tales section, even though, technically speaking, that is not the correct classification for them.

Biographies

Another problem area is that of biographies. In DDC, the number for biographies is 920 or 92 (we remove the zero because, technically speaking, we don't use numbers that end in zero). That puts biographies in between items about history. Many librarians have not been happy with biographies in the middle of history and so have taken the biographical and autobiographical works out of that section and created its own section. Sometimes they will use the full classification number, 920; sometimes they will shorten the number to 92; but often they drop the number completely and simply use the letter "B" or the letters "BIO" (the same way they use "FIC") to designate the biography section. They will then use the first three letters of the last name of the subject of the item; for example, KEN for a biography of John Kennedy, or HAN for a biography of Tom Hanks. This format is the same whether the work is a biography or an autobiography.

Some librarians have argued that separating the biographies from the discipline area does a disservice to the subject of the work. They would argue that biographies of President John Kennedy should be classified under the number 973 for American presidents and that a biography about the actor Tom Hanks should be classified under the number 791 for actors and acting. Again, this brings up the fact that cataloging is an art and not a science and often it is up to catalogers and the knowledge they have of the users in the specific library to determine the best way of dealing with biographical works. Personally, I see lots of merit in putting biographies with the discipline area, as it helps to link the two topics. However, I would venture to say that most of us like to have a biography section to browse when we are thinking that we'd like to read a biography. The choice, once again, is yours, and once again, when you make a decision, you will need to stick to it.

Before we leave biographies, we need to talk about biographies of royalty, because this is the topic that confuses most beginning catalogers. Royalty, and some other famous people, really only have first names. Therefore, biographies about the late Princess Diana will be filed under the letter D for Diana and not the letter W for Wales. Likewise, people who go by only one name, such as the singers Cher and Madonna, will also be filed by their first names. Our users think that way, and this is one case where catalogers agree with their users.

Magazines

Finally, there are always questions about cataloging magazines and journals. Many libraries simply do not catalog them because they think it's too hard. We'll talk later about creating a catalog record for a periodical publication, but for now, we will think only about classification. One could create a classification number for the journal or magazine based on the subject matter; for example, 640.5 for *Good Housekeeping;* 320.05 for *Time Magazine,* or 796.05 for *Sports Illustrated Kids.*[3] Most libraries avoid long classification numbers for periodicals and prefer instead to make something easier for users based mostly on cutter numbers. That's the approach we'll take here. Use something short to keep all of your periodicals together, for example PER or MAG, but select only one designation. Then decide on something short for the title like GHK for *Good Housekeeping,* or TIM for *Time Magazine,* or SIK for *Sports Illustrated Kids.*

Finally, think of a way to show the time of publication as in the month, week, or volume. So *Good Housekeeping* for the month of August 2007 might look like this: PER GHK 8.2007. *Time Magazine* for the week of September 3, 2007 might look like this: PER TIM 09.03.2007. *Sports Illustrated Kids* for August 2007 might look like this: PER SIK 08.2007 or even J PER SIK 08.2007 if you have a separate children's section for magazines for children and young adults. Taking care of periodical publications is a little bit tricky, and we'll cover more issues in later chapters. For now, what you need to know is that this is something that can be done.

CONCLUSION

Classification of books can be seen as being similar to the arrangement of food in a grocery store. We can see how the design of the system goes from the most general to the very specific, like taking a broad view of the store and narrowing it down to items on the shelves. We learn about classification first because it is probably the first thing we want to change when we get our pre-cataloged items in the library. Understanding classification as the foundation to organizing information is our first job as catalogers. Using the Dewey Decimal Classification system cannot be fully explained in a short chapter like this one. However, this chapter should provide you with the rudimentary skills you need to make decisions about changing numbers if necessary. Having a copy of DDC (either the abridged or unabridged editions) while reading through this chapter will help to understand the concepts described here.

It may come as no surprise to learn that Mr. Dewey was a librarian in a university. Being an academic librarian, he probably inferred a certain educational level of his library users. In public and school libraries, a higher level of knowledge cannot be assumed. For librarians who are classifying their items, the index to DDC is most important to help one decide on the small details. For users, the library catalog, subject headings, and key words are important for finding information. In our next chapter, we'll see how subject headings and key words are used to help users find just the right item.

Points to Remember about Chapter 1

- Classification is the act of putting a work into its area of study and, in order to decide on the best DDC number to use, asking ourselves the question, "If someone were to use this work in school, which class would he or she be taking?"
- The Dewey Decimal Classification system defines 10 main classes (or areas of study) into which all knowledge could be divided.
- Those 10 classes are: 000— Computer science, information & general works, 100—Philosophy & psychology, 200—Religion, 300—Social sciences, 400—Language, 500—Science, 600—Technology, 700— Arts & recreation, 800—Literature, 900— History & geography.
- Marks or spaces within the numbers tell us where we can cut off the number if it is too long for the needs of our collection.
- The call number includes the classification number and the cutter number (and often the publication date) for the item.
- Cuttering is the act of creating a cutter number according to the cutter tables, although it is also the term applied to the simple act of using the first three letters of the author's last name.

PROBLEM SET

Assuming that you do not have a Dewey Classification schedule, the exercises here will be limited to the information provided in this chapter and in the OCLC free cutter program.

1. This item is about writing music. Which general number would you assign to this item? (Note: you can only assign a general number; you do not have enough information for a specific number.)
2. This item is about raising cows in Wisconsin and is assigned the number 636.2'009'775. Your collection is small enough to cut off the part about the location (Wisconsin); therefore you want to shorten the number so it represents only raising cows. What will your new number be?
3. The author of the item about raising cows is Arthur C. Benson, and the item was published in 2005. Using the shortened number, cutter it and add the date.

ANSWERS

1. Using the information from Figure 1.2, we would assign the classification number 780 to this item.
2. Even though we're not entirely sure what "009775" means with this number, we do know from Figures 1.3 and 1.4 that the number 636.2 is the classification number assigned to items about "animal husbandry; Ruminants and camel family—bovines—cattle." Cows fit in the bovine classification, and from the use of the apostrophes (') in the number we know that we can cut it off right after the number two, thus modifying the number to 636.2.
3. Using the OCLC cutter program we see that Benson has the number B4431 for the Cutter Four-Figure Table or B4742 for the Cutter-Sanborn Four-Figure Table, giving us the possibility of any of these call numbers:

636.2	636.2
B4431	B4742
2005	2005

NOTES

1. Jon Scieszka and Lane Smith, *Math Curse* (New York: Viking, 1995), p. 2.
2. Ibid., p. 32.

3. The process of building those numbers goes into a detail that is beyond the purpose of this book. However, here is the explanation for those of you who are interested in how the numbers were created. *Good Housekeeping* is a general magazine about ways to run a household, including advice on decorating, cooking, and raising children. Looking in the index of DDC Abridged, one finds the word "household" and follows it to 640 the number for "Home and Family Management." That seems to suit our purposes. We are given the instructions to add the standard subdivisions from Table 1 as needed. Table 1 includes a number for things that are published periodically, as is the case with our magazine. That number is -05. Notice the use of the "-" to show that this number cannot be used alone. We get into a little bit of a potentially confusing problem when we look at the number of zeroes in this number. DDC has a rule to drop zeroes if the number that results will have two or more zeroes next to each other. So our number 640 becomes 64, and to that we add -05 to get 640.5 (putting the decimal point after the third digit). Before you ask, we can only drop the last zero if there is something following it as in the case of our example. We can never have a number that is just two digits (64), except in the case of biographies as explained in this chapter. *Time Magazine* poses another problem. It is a general news magazine. We could have selected 050 for "General serial publications in American English," but that just doesn't capture the news part of the magazine, which is, after all, the purpose of the publication. The number 320 fits better as it represents "Political Science (Politics and Government)." But watch out with this number. The number 320 is further subdivided by .1, .2, and so on. If we dropped the last zero in 320 as we had previously been instructed to do and add the -05 for serial publications, the number 320.5 does not represent serial publication about politics. Rather it represents "political ideologies," which is not what we want at all! DDC has accounted for that problem and instructs us that if we need to use Table 1 standard subdivisions (in this case, -05), we leave in the zero at the end of 320 and we get this number: 320.05. There are always exceptions to the rules in DDC that you have to get used to. Our last example, *Sports Illustrated Kids,* is the most simple. Looking at Figure 1.2, we can see that 790 is the classification number for "Sports, Games, and Entertainment." Going to DDC itself, we see that the number for general sports, "Athletic and Outdoor Sports and Games" is 796. Add our old friend -05 and we get the number 796.05. Notice we did not drop the zero because the number 796 does not end in a zero.

CHAPTER 2

What You Need to Know about Subject and Key Word Headings

Dewey designed the classification system around disciplines of study such as zoology and animal husbandry. But most of the time when people are looking for information they want something more specific than a broad discipline, or they may not even know what the discipline is that they are thinking about (who knew that a book about taking care of a pet cat would be classified under animal husbandry?). That's why understanding subject headings and key word searching comes in handy.

Let's go back to our grocery store and pretend we're looking for canned and fresh peas. We have two different classifications: "canned" and "fresh." We also have the division of "vegetables" for both of our items. We go to the grocery clerk and ask for these things. But we have something specific in mind, so we don't ask where the canned goods (discipline) are located, and we don't even ask where the canned vegetables (division) are located; we ask where the canned peas (subject) are located. Following the same logic for our fresh peas we can see that our subject headings are more specific than our classifications and that by asking for those specific items we are more likely to be led to exactly the right place in the store and to the correct shelf than if we asked for the more general canned or fresh goods. This saves us and our clerk time and results in a more positive shopping experience. However, we have to be careful here.

What if we are looking for green peas and the grocery clerk leads us the black-eyed peas? They are, after all, both called peas, but they are also both very different from each other. We see here that the words we choose to describe items impact how easily our users can find the items they seek.

CONTROLLED VOCABULARIES AND KEY WORDS

Subject headings are lists of words that have been agreed upon by an organization or committee that says "this is the word we are going to use for this concept." Subject headings lists are referred to as **controlled vocabulary**. That is, the organization or committee agrees to use the word "peas" instead of, for example, "legumes," or "Pisum sativum" to cover all kinds of peas and decides that any item about peas (regardless of the type) will be given the subject heading "peas." Not so with key words.

Key words come from the item itself. The vocabulary is not controlled by any authority. So if the can says "peas," then we find our peas, but if the can says "legumes," then we won't find what we're looking for. Here's another example: Let's say we have our peas but now we want some butter to put on them. If we have a subject heading, for example "butter," that covers the yellow stuff one puts on hot peas, be that butter, margarine, or buttery spread, then we will find all of the different products and could make our selection according to our exact needs. But key words are any words used to describe the item, and therefore if we look for "butter" we will find only butter and will miss knowing that there is also something very much like butter except it has a lower fat content: margarine.

In the library world, the difference between subject headings and key words can be confusing to our users who are used to the uncontrolled world of Internet searching. Let's look at an example I like to use to show the difference between key word and subject heading searching—surfing. Try to follow along the steps described here with your local library catalog. Most online catalogs allow one to search subject headings or key words. So type in the word surfing and click the key word search. I recently conducted this search using a statewide library catalog of a state that includes large academic libraries as well as small rural public libraries. In doing this I retrieved 610 hits for items that covered everything from learning how to surf the big waves of Hawaii to surviving in the world of big business to learning how to use the Internet for home-schooled children. What were your results? Now try the search again, but this time click on the subject search option. Using the same database, when I conducted the subject search I got 270 items. Even though they were not all non-fiction works, every item had to do with standing on a board on a wave in the ocean. What were your results? Were your results better using the subject search?

Is there a benefit to key word searching? What if you really wanted to know about surfing the Internet? Try searching "surfing Internet" (without quotation marks) with a key word search. What happens? What happens if you try this as a subject search?

When I tried this with my big statewide catalog, I ended up with 75 items using the key word search and zero items using a subject search. Zero items! Now that would be a frustrating and misleading result for the library user. In this case our search is more productive using a key word instead of a subject heading search.

We can see here that conducting this search using the subject heading "surfing" can be much more efficient than conducting the search using the key word search option. But we can miss things too. What if the cataloger created a catalog record for an item and used the broader subject heading "aquatic sports" instead of the more specific subject heading "surfing," even if surfing was in the title of the item? In this case we'd miss the item doing a subject search but would find it in a key word search because somewhere in the catalog record is the word "surfing." There are pros and cons to both subject and key word searching, which is why it is so important that you as librarians and your users understand both concepts. Even as catalogers there is a need to be teachers as well as librarians and teach our users why we need both subject as well as key word searching skills.

WHAT ARE *LCSH* AND *SEARS*?

Two standard lists of subject headings are used in public and school libraries: *LCSH* and *Sears*. LCSH stands for **Library of Congress Subject Headings**. Because this list has come from the Library of Congress, it is treated with a great deal of respect. The staff at the Library of Congress is responsible for a great deal of cataloging in the United States. However, the list of subject headings was originally created by the Library of Congress to provide subject access to items needed by members of the U.S. Congress. It was not originally created for the general public and therefore reflects, again, an academic approach to retrieving information. Over the past few years, there has been a concerted effort to change the scientific terms to the more popular terms, but one can still see the academic influence, especially when there is a big difference between scientific and words used by the general public. *LCSH* is big (currently five volumes) and expensive (almost $300) so it is not commonly found in school or smaller public libraries.

Recognizing the problem with using *LCSH* in a school or smaller public library, a cataloger named Minnie Earl Sears put together a subject headings list that focused on the words and phrases used by the general public to search for information. A brief biography of Ms. Sears is available from H.W. Wilson Company, the publishing house where she spent much of her professional life and where she published her subject headings list (see: http://www.hwwilson.com/news/news_2_6_04.htm#story). The subject list, first published in 1923, was renamed the ***Sears List of Subject Headings*** (*Sears*) in 1950, and is still in use today. School and small public libraries find the single volume of *Sears* easier to use and much less expensive than the five volumes of *LCSH*. One of the benefits of *Sears* over *LCSH* is that it is quicker to recognize changes in popular culture and so is easier to use with younger library users. Additionally, many more vendors who supply cataloging to libraries are recognizing that many librarians use the *Sears* subject headings and so are providing those headings along with the Library of Congress headings. Despite their different developments, over the years, the two lists have become closer and closer in nature. Headings in *LCSH* are changing from academic to more vernacular terms, and *Sears* is expanding. It is still helpful to have the one volume *Sears* work handy, but technically speaking subject headings can be assigned using only the online version of *LCSH* (see http://authorities.loc.gov/). It isn't easy to use the online version without a good knowledge of the structure of subject headings, but it can be done.

STRUCTURE OF SUBJECT HEADINGS LISTS

Both *LCSH* and *Sears* are arranged in alphabetical order with connections to the vocabulary words in terms of broader, narrower, and related words as well as words that users might think of but that are not used on the lists. Let's go back to our surfing subject heading. To follow this discussion, take a look at the subject headings site for the Library of Congress at: http://authorities.loc.gov/ and click on the heading "Search Authorities" to enter the subject headings catalog. In the search bar type the word "surfing" (without the quotation marks). We see the red and orange button that reads "Authorized & References." This is a good thing to see. It means that we have a word that *LCSH* recognizes as an authorized heading. Before we look at this example, click the "New Search" button at the top of the screen and type in the words "daddy longlegs." Notice in this case the button reads only "References." This means that "daddy longlegs" is not a valid subject heading but has a reference to the correct heading. We'll come back to daddy longlegs, but let's click on the new search button and try one more search. Type in the two words "gold finches." Now we see that nothing matches our search. Not only do we not have a valid subject heading, but there isn't even any reference to something close to gold finches. What we might not know is that the correct term is one word: "goldfinches." An experienced bird watcher might know that it's one word, but someone who is just learning about birds might not know this and would think that the library has nothing about this pretty little songbird. So we have three responses to our search: valid, referenced, and invalid.

Example—Surfing

Let's go back to our valid heading, surfing, and see what we can learn. First, the database we are using is the **authority file**. This means that it is not a catalog record but information about words and phrases that are recognized by the Library of Congress as the correct and valid words and phrases to use in cataloging items. The authority file can include subject headings and also names of people (it tells us to use Bill Clinton, not William Jefferson Clinton); names of corporations (New York [NY] Fire Dept., not FDNY); sports teams (Seattle SuperSonics [Basketball team] not Sonics); and so on. Searching the authority file helps us to know that the words we're entering into a catalog record and using when doing a search are correct or valid words. In cataloging there is very little we can just make up as we go along. Using the authoritative terms is important for standardized cataloging practice.

When we look at the display for our surfing search we have two ways of looking at our result; MARC display or Labelled display. The MARC display looks like some kind of mathematical nightmare. We'll discuss the MARC display in chapter 4. Click on the button for labelled display or follow along using Figure 2.1 as we look to see what goes into a subject heading. To explain what we see: The LC Control Number is the number given to the authority record. We know it is a subject heading because the number begins with "sh." The LC Class Number is the classification number, using not DDC but the Library of Congress Classification system. We can see that this number is very different from the DDC numbers we got used to seeing in chapter 1.

Finally we get to the heading itself: Surfing. The "used for/see from" phrase means that these words are not the right words for a work about surfing. But notice that no distinction is made between body surfing and board surfing, which may upset the surfing enthusiast, but that's the way it goes. We also have the "search also under" which means that this is also a term that covers surfing but also includes other water sports. As an aside, this is a good example of the difference between *LCSH* and *Sears*. Where *LCSH* uses "aquatic sports" as a subject heading, *Sears* uses "water sports." Which term is your user more likely to search? The "used for/see from" and "search also under" are what we call in the library world cross references.

A **cross reference** means that in the searching system (card or computer) there is a reference or lead from one term to another. The reference can be from an invalid term, in this case body surfing, to the valid terms, surfing; or from a broader term, aquatic sports, to a more specific or narrower term, surfing. In an online catalog, the user may never see the cross reference. In this case the user might type in the search

LC Control Number: sh 85130757
LC Class Number: GV839.5 GV839.7
HEADING: Surfing
Used For/See From: Body surfing
                    Surf riding
                    Surfboard riding
                    Surfboarding
                    Surfriding
Search Also Under: Aquatic sports
Found In: LC database, 6/22/95 (surfboarding)

Figure 2.1.   Labelled display for the Library of Congress subject heading: Surfing (captured December 1, 2008).

(for example, surfboard riding) and the computer program would automatically take the user to records with the correct subject heading (surfing). Some systems will have a screen appear that directs the user to the correct search. Unhelpful systems simply reply that there are no items with that subject heading. In this case the system is unhelpful or the librarian has failed to set up the cross reference. Cross references, like mostly everything in the catalog, do not happen automatically. Someone has to tell the computer what to do; that is, someone has to set up the cross reference. We'll talk more about this in chapter 4 when we take a brief exploration into the world of authority records. For now, let's look again at our surfing subject heading example.

With our example we can see that "Aquatic sports" (or "Water sports" for *Sears* users) covers more than just surfing. It is broader in scope. In the print world of *LCSH,* we would see BT, NT, and RT as designations for alternatives to our subject heading. In an attempt to be more user friendly, the Library of Congress uses "search also under." It's less mysterious, but we don't get a sense of the relationship between "aquatic sports" and "surfing." Later in this chapter we'll see an example heading from *Sears* that displays all of the relationships.

Example—Daddy Longlegs

For now, let's get back to the other subject searches we conducted and find out why they were less successful than our search for "surfing." Going back to the Library of Congress Authority records database (http://authorities.loc.gov/), let's again search the words "daddy longlegs." We see two things. On the first line of our results we see the term with a red button to the left of it that reads "References." Before we click on that button, notice the next line down also reads "daddy longlegs"; but this time, to its left, we see the "good" red button that reads "Authorized Heading." Remember from our "surfing" example that this means this is a valid subject heading. Before you get confused, read across that row and see that this type of heading is "LC subject headings for Children."

When it became clear that *LCSH* was being used beyond the original intended use as information retrieval for members of Congress, the Library of Congress created a much smaller and much simpler list of subject headings for its LC/AC program. "AC" means annotated card and was a system for assigning subject headings to children's materials. So on this screen we see that kids can search for the subject of daddy longlegs but adults cannot. This used to be important when adults and children had their own card catalogs in the library. Today, with combined electronic catalogs, users will not know if they are using a children's or adult subject heading. The adult looking for something about daddy longlegs may be unhappy and confused, however, if the subject search "daddy longlegs" results only in retrieving children's materials. Again, we see we have to do some teaching to help the user find just what he or she is looking for.

Let's find out what the proper "adult" search term is. Click on the "References" button. We come to a screen that offers us three choices: the authority record or to see Pholcidae or Opiliones. If we click on the authority record we see those same two scientific names. Clicking on either of those names will show two authority records (make sure you're looking at the labelled display) that show "daddy longlegs" as an invalid subject heading. Figure 2.2 shows the two authority records side-by-side for easy comparison.

I had to look up those two scientific names and talk to an expert on spiders to find out that they are actually two different types of spiders and the child's daddy longlegs is really the adult's pholcidae. This example shows us a few things: (1) that the Library of Congress has developed two sets of subject headings and that the headings used for Congress and the rest of the adult world are not always the same as those used for children; (2) that an adult using a term considered to be a children's term may have problems finding the right item; and (3) that cross references are important ways to aid in the searching process.

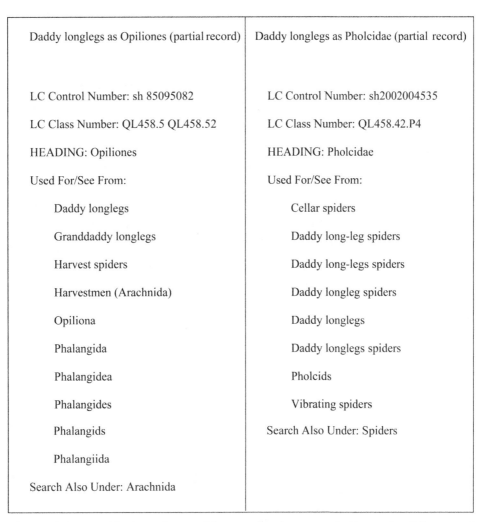

Daddy longlegs as Opiliones (partial record)	Daddy longlegs as Pholcidae (partial record)
LC Control Number: sh 85095082	LC Control Number: sh2002004535
LC Class Number: QL458.5 QL458.52	LC Class Number: QL458.42.P4
HEADING: Opiliones	HEADING: Pholcidae
Used For/See From:	Used For/See From:
Daddy longlegs	Cellar spiders
Granddaddy longlegs	Daddy long-leg spiders
Harvest spiders	Daddy long-legs spiders
Harvestmen (Arachnida)	Daddy longleg spiders
Opiliona	Daddy longlegs
Phalangida	Daddy longlegs spiders
Phalangidea	Pholcids
Phalangides	Vibrating spiders
Phalangids	Search Also Under: Spiders
Phalangiida	
Search Also Under: Arachnida	

Figure 2.2.   Daddy Longlegs subject authority records from the Library of Congress (captured December 1, 2008).

Example—Gold Finches

Our last subject search is the one for "gold finches." Recall when we conducted this search we retrieved no information at all. A cross reference here would have come in handy. If you have a system that allows you to put in your own authority records, you might consider creating one for the real subject heading, "goldfinches" (one word) to help the searcher who is not an expert in bird names to know that the proper term for the bird is one word and not two words. Some systems are very sophisticated and will suggest to the user the proper term, but many systems for smaller libraries are not that sophisticated.

USING *SEARS* AS A CATALOGING TOOL

As we know, the *LCSH* database is available for free on the Internet, but just because it is there for free does not make it the best resource for our purposes. The advantage to having the *Sears* book on your desk is that you can easily move back and forth between subject headings to decide between two headings, whether the broader heading is better to use than the narrower heading, or if it is all right to establish a specific heading. Even though *Sears* and *LCSH* are based on similar theories of construction, that construction is not evident using *LCSH* online. Additionally, *Sears* has the advantage of showing us the DDC number that would go with the subject heading, which is a big plus in terms of usefulness! With these two thoughts in mind, it is worth exploring how to use the *Sears* book.

Figure 2.3 shows us what the subject heading "motorcycles" looks like in *Sears*. Notice that we have reference abbreviations (BT, NT, RT) that we've seen earlier in this chapter. Notice too the number "629.227," which is the DDC number for Cycles.

Taking this apart step by step, we see, on the first line, that "Motorcycles" is in bold print. This is important to *Sears*; it means that this is a valid subject heading. The designation "(May subdiv. Geog.)" means that if you had a large enough collection and you

Motorcycles (May subdiv. Geog.)   **629.227**

UF   Motor cycles

SA   specific makes and models of motorcycles [to be added as needed]

BT   **Bicycles**

NT   **Antique and vintage motorcycles**

       Minibikes

RT   **Motorcycling**

Figure 2.3.   *Sears* entry for motorcycles (p. 503).

had two items, one about motorcycles in Japan and one about motorcycles in the United States, you could create a subject heading to bring out the geographic information in the subject heading. Our collection is probably not large enough to need this additional information, but if it was you could create the heading (for example, Motorcycles—Japan) and it would be a legal and valid heading. Not every subject heading can be subdivided by geographical location. That note is important to us, but it is not always clear in the *LCSH* online, which is another good reason for having the *Sears* book in front of you. The last thing we see on the first line is the DDC number, 629.227. This is the big advantage of using the *Sears* book instead of *LCSH*. You can't depend totally on this information, but it can be used to help you make decisions about assigning classification numbers.

If you have a copy of DDC abridged, take a look at that number. Seeing how that number is constructed will help us to understand the rest of the subject heading information. The number 629.227 is the one used for "Cycles." Thus bicycles and motorcycles are classified under the same number. If you are in a library, go to the technology (600) section and see if you can find at least the number 629. Notice the types of items that are put together on the shelf: motorcycles, bicycles, cars, trucks, etc.

Moving down to the second line we see "UF Motor cycles" (UF stands for Use For). Notice that this line is not in bold print; this line provides instructions to the cataloger and is not a valid heading. It says, "Do not use motor cycles; instead use motorcycles"; that is, the subject heading is one word and not two. The next line also provides instructions for the cataloger, and here is where *Sears* is really different from *LCSH*. The SA means See Also, and in this case we are told that we can see also (use also as a subject heading) the name of the motorcycle. So if we have an item about Harley-Davidson motorcycles, we have permission here to create our own subject heading for Harley-Davidson. *LCSH* does not give us that kind of permission without going through the formal process of adding or changing a heading.

Next we see BT, NT, and RT, and, as promised earlier in the chapter, we will now find out what that means. BT stands for broader term. In our example we see that the word "Bicycles" is given as a broader term, or subject heading, for motorcycles. This is true because a motorcycle is a bicycle, that is to say a two-wheeled vehicle, with a motor. However, it is highly unlikely that the user who asks for something about bicycles is really looking for motorcycles. At any rate, *Sears,* and actually *LCSH* as well, treat motorcycles as a kind of subset of bicycles. In practice, we don't really have to worry too much about this.

The other headings however, the NTs and RTs, will be important to us. NT is used as an abbreviation for narrower term. In our example we see two narrower terms: Antique and vintage motorcycles and Minibikes. It is very possible that the person using the subject heading search "motorcycles" may in fact be looking for something about antique motorcycles. A good card or online system should be able to lead the user to this more specific subject heading. Where narrower terms are subsets of our subject term, the RT, or related term, points the user to something that is at the same level. In a way it is saying, well if you want to know about the motorcycle, you may also be interested in the people who ride them or the art of riding a motorcycle. Going back to our grocery store, we may think about related terms in this way; if you are interested in fresh peas, it may also interest you to know that the store also carries canned and frozen peas.

SPECIAL TYPES OF SUBJECT HEADINGS

We have seen how a thing like a motorcycles or an activity like surfing can be used as subject headings, but what if you have an item about a person, like a U.S. president, or a place, like the city of New York, or a thing, like the Titanic? *Sears* has a section in the book that shows how to create those kinds of headings by using an example as a model. *LCSH,* on the other hand, provides us with most of the headings we would need to make in these situations. Go to *LCSH* online (http://authorities.loc. gov/) and look up George W. Bush, New York City, and Titanic.

In looking up a person's name using the *LCSH* online site, the first thing we notice is that we have to look up the name using the last name first. If we type in the search "george w bush" we get people whose last name is George. So let's try bush as the first word in our search. Notice that in searching this page online, we don't have to worry about using capital letters. This search page is not "case sensitive," which means it doesn't care if you ask it to search for "Bush" or for "bush." Another feature of this page is that we don't have to put in any punctuation. So now let's try "bush george w" and see what we get. Figure 2.4 shows a part of the display of our search results.

This chart gives us a lot to think about when we are looking at it. The first column tells us that this is the number of headings found for our search. Figure 2.4 shows us only the first five headings found for our search. The second row tells us how many "Bib Records" are connected to that heading. That phrase "Bib Records" is short for bibliographic records. We'll find out in the next chapter the full definition of bibliographic records. For now, it is enough to say that this column tells us how many times this heading is found in the Library of Congress catalog database. The final column tells us what kind of subject heading this is. We are familiar with LC (Library of Congress) subject headings and LC subject headings for children, but the Library of Congress recognizes and uses many other different types of subject headings. For our purposes, we are happy to see "LC subject headings" or "LC subject headings for children." Now let's look at the results themselves.

The first two results have little "Authorized Heading" buttons, and that's good for us because we remember that this means these are good headings to use. The other results do not have those buttons, but do not worry; this will be explained very soon. Looking at our first two subject headings, we see two different George W. Bush people. We see a Bush, George W. who lived from 1824–1900 and a Bush, George W. (George Walker) who was born in 1946 and is still alive. The second Bush is the one we want to look at. Compare row numbers two and three in the figure. Notice the only difference between the two is that one is set up for *LCSH* headings and the other for *LC/AC* headings. We've seen how these two headings can be different from each other, and now we see that they can also be the same.

#	Bib Records	*select icon in first column to...* View Authority Headings/References	Type of Heading
[Authorized Heading] 1	0	Bush, George W., 1824-1900	LC subject headings
[Authorized Heading] 2	314	Bush, George W. (George Walker), 1946-	LC subject headings
3	19	Bush, George W. (George Walker), 1946-	LC subject headings for children
4	2	Bush, George W. (George Walker), 1946- Anecdotes.	LC subject headings
5	2	Bush, George W. (George Walker), 1946- Career in the military.	LC subject headings

Figure 2.4.   Search results for "bush george w" on *LSCH* online subject authorities database (captured December 1, 2008).

Now let's look at rows four and five. The words that follow Bush's name, "Anecdotes" and "Career in the military," are **subheadings** of our subject heading. If you search for any of our U.S. presidents, you will find that these subheadings are the same for most of them. Subheadings are not subject headings, but they help us to further focus our search. So in row four, we're not just interested in Bush; we want to find something that is a collection of stories about him. Anecdotes are not the same as biographies. They don't attempt to tell the story of the person's life; rather, they tell stories about the person. In this search, we know that there are two works that are anecdotes about Bush. Row five tells us there are also two works that refer to Bush's military career. Remember that subject headings tell us what the work is *about*. However, a work may be about more than one thing. So we could have a work that includes anecdotes about Bush's military career. In this case one work would have two subject headings. The number of subject headings that can be applied to each item is in a sense without limit. In reality, however, items usually get no more than three to five subject headings. So we see here that these are some of the subject headings that can be assigned to works that are about George W. Bush. These are not works that are written by him; these are works that tell us something about him. Not all works that are about people are biographies. For example, a work about the 2000 presidential election in the United States might in fact have the presidential candidates George W. Bush and Al Gore as subject headings even though the work is not a biography of either man. Including Bush and Gore as subject headings tells our library users that the work includes information about the two men.

One more thing to say about searching for people as subjects is that royal people are treated differently than the rest of us. We search for Elizabeth, Diana, Charles, etc., by their first names because, as noted in chapter 1, they don't really have last names. If we are cataloging items about these people, we need to look them up because there will be more to their names, as we will soon see. However, for our users who complain that we don't have anything about Elizabeth, Queen of England, it will be enough for us to say, "Let me take you to the biography section, she will be under the letter E for Elizabeth."

What does a royal heading look like? Let's find out! Go to the *LCSH* online database and look up Elizabeth II. This is what we find: Elizabeth II, Queen of Great Britain, 1926–. How about her husband, Philip; what does his subject heading look like? Turns out he is a lot harder to find than Elizabeth was. We can't just look for "philip"; there are far too many of them. If you try "philip prince" you will find what you are looking for: Philip, Prince, consort of Elizabeth II, Queen of Great Britain, 1921–. Actually the structure for Philip's subject heading is exactly the same as that of Elizabeth's. The problem is the user has to know that Philip is not the King of Great Britain (or England), but rather a prince and consort (husband) of Elizabeth II.

We have seen how subject headings work for items about specific people. What about our next quest—a work about New York City. Works about places are a little tricky and often do not work out in a way that seems logical to our users. Remember that these subject headings were created first as an in-house system for the Library of Congress for members of Congress to use; not for the local person in your library. With that in mind, type in "new york city" in the *LCSH* database search bar. We recognize right away that little red button labeled "References" that tells us this is not the right way to look up this place. So when a library user comes up to you to complain that you don't have any books about New York City, be patient and know that it is not entirely your user's fault for not being able to find the right item.

A click on that red Reference button and following the links to the "authority record" will tell us that the right subject heading is "New York (N.Y.)" This makes us wonder if other cities follow the same pattern. For example, what if we want to look up Seattle, Washington? *LCSH* tells us that the correct heading is "Seattle (Wash.)." We almost have a pattern. Let's try, Madison, Wisconsin. Here we come to a halt. If we type in "madison wisconsin" we get no results, not even a red Reference button. If we type in "madison" we get a reference to a person named Madison. So let's try something similar to our Seattle example; let's try "madison wi" and see what happens.

What is happening is that we have to figure out how the Library of Congress abbreviates the names of the states. Washington State is "Wash." But Wisconsin is "Wis." How do we know which abbreviation to use? The U.S. Postal Service is actually the answer to our question, almost. In the old days, perhaps even before the introduction of the zip code way back in the 1960s, state abbreviations at the time were two, three, and four letters. Washington became Wash.; Wisconsin became Wis.; Georgia became Ga.; and so on. Knowing how to look up a city may be second nature to a more veteran librarian, but for those of you who don't remember the 1960s, a list of state abbreviations used to find city names is provided for you here in Figure 2.5.

State Name	State Abbreviation	State Name	State Abbreviation
Alabama	Ala.	Montana	Mont.
Alaska	Alaska	Nebraska	Neb.
Arizona	Ariz.	Nevada	Nev.
Arkansas	Ark.	New Hampshire	N.H.
California	Calif.	New Jersey	N.J.
Colorado	Colo.	New Mexico	N.M.
Connecticut	Conn.	New York	N.Y.
Delaware	Del.	North Carolina	N.C.
Florida	Fla.	North Dakota	N.D.
Georgia	Ga.	Ohio	Ohio
Hawaii	Hawaii	Oklahoma	Okla.
Idaho	Idaho	Oregon	Or.
Illinois	Ill.	Pennsylvania	Pa.
Indiana	Ind.	Rhode Island	R.I.
Iowa	Iowa	South Carolina	S.C.
Kansas	Kan.	South Dakota	S.D.
Kentucky	Ky.	Tennessee	Tenn.
Louisiana	La.	Texas	Tex.
Maine	Me.	Utah	Utah
Maryland	Md.	Vermont	Vt.
Massachusetts	Mass.	Virginia	Va.
Michigan	Mich.	Washington	Wash.
Minnesota	Minn.	West Virginia	W.Va.
Mississippi	Miss.	Wisconsin	Wis.
Missouri	Mo.	Wyoming	Wyo.

Figure 2.5.   List of U.S. state abbreviations. Note that not every state is abbreviated.

With this list, you should be able to look up the name of any U.S. city for the purposes of subject headings. When you do look up the city, the search will be the name of the city and the abbreviation of the state in parentheses. For example: little rock (ark). For abbreviations for cities outside of the United States, you will have to use trial and error.

To look up a geographical location, such as the Grand Canyon in Arizona or the Florida Everglades, you can usually use the same process as looking up a city. For example, to find the Grand Canyon, type the search "grand canyon (ariz)" and you will usually get what you are looking for. Usually but not always! Try now to search "florida everglades (fla)" and what do you find? You find a reference to "Everglades (Fla.)." In all honesty that does make a certain amount of sense. After all it is a little redundant to say Florida Everglades Florida (as if the Florida Everglades would be located some place besides Florida!). However, think of how many of your users would actually look under "Everglades." That is simply not how we think about that place. This is a good example of how a key word search might be more productive for our users than a subject search.

Our last special subject search is for a thing. People do want to look up things like the Titanic, the Empire State Building, or Wrigley Field. It takes a long explanation to understand how catalogers talk about these kinds of things. For our purposes, what we really want to know is if our users look up Empire State Building, will they find what we have on that subject? The answer is yes . . . sort of. The truth is that the location of the thing or the specification of what that thing is, is usually included in the subject heading. For example, in looking up "titanic" we find that the real subject heading is "Titanic (Steamship)," in looking up "empire state building" we find that the real subject heading is "Empire State Building (New York, N.Y.)," and in looking up "wrigley field" we find that the real subject heading is "Wrigley Field (Chicago, Ill.)." The point is that our users should be able to find what they are looking for by searching under the name of the thing even if they don't get it exactly right.

CONCLUSION

In chapter 1, we found out that our collections are organized according to the classification of information and that classification is based on the areas of studies (or classes) that the works are produced for. In this chapter, we have learned that besides classifying our works, we can give them subject headings that tell our users what the items are about. Subject headings are controlled lists of words or phrases, and the two most commonly used lists in school and public libraries are *LCSH* and *Sears*. We also learned that online catalogs of our collections allow users to find things based on key word searching. Key words may or may not have anything to do with what the items are about. Key words come directly from the catalog record, and so searching by key word may result in getting a list of items that do not have anything to do with what the user needs. Usually a combination of key word and subject searching will help our users find the right items.

We see too that *LCSH* and *Sears* headings are constructed in a similar fashion, working their way from broadest to narrowest term and leaving room for individual librarians to add their own words as needed for their users. As mentioned in the previous section, Ms. Sears recognized that her list could not be comprehensive, and so she had the list published with large margins for individual libraries to add vocabulary as needed.

Making changes to *LCSH* is a much more formal process. Librarians can go to the cataloging site for the Library of Congress and complete a form for correcting or changing subject headings (see: http://www.loc.gov/catdir/pcc/prop/proposal.html). You need to provide a good reason for suggesting the change. Reasons for change are based on "literary warrant." That is, if there are enough publications on the subject and it is a subject that will not go away quickly (it's not a fad) then the suggestion will be taken to committee and a decision made on how to respond to the suggestion. Changes are not taken lightly, as they impact libraries across North America and even around the world. Imagine what would happen if canning factories had to stop printing labels for pineapple if it suddenly became apple of the pine cone! Similar chaos happens when dramatic changes are made to subject headings, which is not to say that changes don't happen (just look at the weekly list of changes on the LC site: http://www.loc.gov/aba/cataloging/subject/weeklylists/), but there has to be a good reason to make the change.

Headings used by the Library of Congress are slowly changing to be more like natural language, and they are available to look up for free from the Library of Congress web site. However, the *Sears* headings were created expressly for smaller collections like those found in school and small public libraries. You might find that having a hard copy of *Sears* available to check for appropriate subject headings is more efficient than going to the Library of Congress site.

Organizing works in a library is more than describing what the item is about; we also need to describe the item itself. This physical description is explained in the next chapter.

Points to Remember about Chapter 2

- Subject headings are used to tell us what the item is about.
- Key words are different from subject headings for two reasons: There is no official list of key words and they may have nothing to do with what the item is about.
- The two most commonly used subject headings lists are the *Library of Congress List of Subject Headings (LCSH)* and the *Sears List of Subject Headings (Sears)*.
- *LCSH* is available for free online, which makes it economical and convenient, but *Sears* is created expressly for school and small public libraries, which makes it easier to use for us and our library users.
- Often items will have more than one subject heading but usually not more than three to five headings.

PROBLEM SET

Use the Library of Congress Subject Authorities site (http://authorities.loc.gov/) to find the headings for these problems.

1. You have a book about high school dropouts in the United States. Can you find two subject headings for this book?
2. You have a book about Disney World in Florida. Can you find two subject headings to use?
3. You have a movie about pilots of World War II. What would the subject headings be?

ANSWERS

1. Searching "high school dropouts" leads us to a couple of options. First, we see that we do have an authorized heading. So far, so good. Clicking on the red button and the link to show the authority record, this is what the labelled view looks like:

HEADING:	High school dropouts
Used For/See From:	Secondary school dropouts
Search Also Under:	Dropouts
	High school students

(Retrieved from *LCSH* authorities database, December 1, 2008)

We can use "High school dropouts" as one subject heading. The instructions: "Search Also Under" tell us that we can also use "Dropouts" and "High school students" as second and even third subject headings. But we have not been able to show that this is a book about high school dropouts in the United States. If we go back to the search results, we can see a long list underneath "high school dropouts." The first one reads, "High school dropouts Africa." This gives us an idea. If we can add the country of Africa to the subject heading, can we also add the country, United States? If we go back to the search page and type the search "high school dropouts united states" we will find that in fact that is a good heading, so lucky us! Actually, if we try our other headings as well, it turns out that we can add "United States" to all of them (that's not always the case, so it is always good practice to look it up). Here then are our choices for this problem:

High school dropouts. United States.

Dropouts. United States.

High school students. United States.

We would have to know more about the book and our collection before we made a final decision about these subject headings. If most of our items were about the United States, it might be overkill to add the subdivision "United States" to these headings. We might decide that just the subject heading "High school dropouts" (with or without the addition of "United States") is really good enough for our users. Much of our decision would be based on the contents of the item. We would look through the table of contents and maybe the index to decide if more subject headings are needed.

2. If we follow past practice and search for "disney world fla" (using the correct abbreviation for Florida) we find that we have an incorrect heading. Following the path to the correct heading, we get this:

HEADING:	Walt Disney World (Fla.)
Used For/See From:	Disney World (Fla.)
	Magic Kingdom (Fla.)
Search Also Under:	Amusement parks. Florida
	EPCOT Center (Fla.)

(Retrieved from LCSH authorities database, December 1, 2008)

This information tells us that the correct heading is Walt Disney World (Fla.); that we cannot use Disney World (Fla.) or Magic Kingdom (Fla.); and that we can also use Amusement parks. Florida or EPCOT Center (Fla.). If our book is also about the EPCOT Center then we would want to make sure to use that as a subject heading. However, it might also be nice to use the Amusement parks subject heading. You can imagine in your own catalog that if you had many items about different amusement parks, it might be nice to pull them altogether under the broad subject heading "Amusement parks." Here then are our answers for this problem:

Walt Disney World (Fla.)

Amusement parks. Florida.

3. This is by far the most difficult of the problems, and it probably took you some time, and maybe even a little frustration, to come to some conclusions. It was given here on purpose to show that wars are difficult for our users to find because they simply are not named the same way by the Library of Congress as they are for the rest of us. We talk about the Civil War, but the Library of Congress calls it "United States–History–Civil War, 1861–1865." We talk about World War II, but the Library of Congress calls it "World War, 1939–1945." We talk about the Vietnam War, but the Library of Congress calls it "Vietnam War, 1961–1975." Likewise, the war in Iraq is called "Iraq War, 2003–" by the Library of Congress. Well at least those last two are fairly close to the way we think about them. The point is that

sometimes your users will get frustrated, and you need to understand their frustrations. This problem was also included because there are different kinds of pilots, and you are going to have to work your way from "pilot" to "air pilot" and you'll have to steer your users in that direction as well. So how do we do that?

Let's start with what would seem very logical to us (and our users): "pilots world war ii" or even "world war ii pilots." Those searches are completely useless (and will be for your users as well). Notice, however, that it does appear that "World War II" is a viable heading. Be warned that the results from this search are leading you to authoritative headings for titles of items and not for subject headings. If this is confusing to you, imagine how your users are feeling right now! This is a time when you will simply have to train your customers to use the right heading.

When faced with a long search, try cutting it down into smaller parts. Search first under "pilots." The result is that "pilots," according to the Library of Congress, are the people who steer boats. The Library of Congress provides us with a link from "Pilots (Aeronautics)" to "Air pilots." This looks promising. If we search under "air pilots" we find out that "Air Pilots" is a good heading to use, but a narrower heading, "Air pilots, Military," might be a better heading. Depending on our item, we could even use "Air pilots, Military" and add a place, such as "United States," if we have such a specific focus. But for our users and the size of our collection, it might be enough to just use "Air pilots, Military." But how do we incorporate World War II to our heading? Maybe we need a separate heading? In the start of our explanation to this problem, we already learned not to look under "world war ii" but to search "world war 1939–1945." So we do that and our results are shown in Figure 2.6, which has been slightly abridged for the sake of our discussion.

Given this information, we could well be happy with "World War, 1939–1945—Aerial operations" as a broad subject heading that incorporates both the war and the pilots. We can also keep the "Air pilots, Military" subject heading. But something is bothering us. We are trying hard to think of a user in our library who would say, "Excuse me, do you have any videos on World War, 1939–1945 Aerial operations?" So we might be happy with "World War, 1939–1945" and "Air pilots, Military" or we might hope that there is something even better. We also see that the heading for Japanese air operations has a link to other references. We click on the red button and see a reference for "Kamikaze pilots" as a narrower term. If that applies to our video, we might want to use that heading as well. If we go back to our search under "world war 1939–1945" we also notice that there is page after page of subject headings that begin with that search including "World War 1939–1945—Air operations." We're not exactly sure what the different is between "aerial operations" and "air operations," but we think that "air"

#	Bib Records	Authority Headings/References	Type of Heading
Authorized Heading	2171	World War, 1939-1945	LC subject headings
Authorized Heading	69	World War, 1939-1945	LC subject headings for children
	139	World War, 1939-1945 Addresses, sermons, etc.	LC subject headings
	3	World War, 1939-1945 Aegean Islands (Greece and Turkey)	LC subject headings
	1	World War, 1939-1945 Aerial operations, American.	LC subject headings
	1	World War, 1939-1945 Aerial operations, British.	LC subject headings
Authorized & References	1	World War, 1939-1945 Aerial operations, Japanese.	LC subject headings

Figure 2.6. Search results for world war 1939–1945 (captured December 1, 2008).

might be friendlier than "aerial." It actually takes a bit of research to find out that the heading we really want to use is "aerial operations," so that's what we will use. We hope that our customers will use a key word search to find this video, because we suspect that the headings we have come up with ("Air pilots, Military" and "World War, 1939–1945—Aerial operations") are not clear enough to help out our users. This problem is a good illustration of when a key word search might well be more beneficial than a subject heading search.

CHAPTER 3

What You Need to Know about Description

Let's go back to the grocery store and ask our clerk this question: "Do you have those things that are long and kind of curvy and you peel them to get to the white part that you eat?" In this question we have given the clerk a description of the item we are looking for. We have not described the item in terms of what it is about or what it tastes like, but what it looks like. This is a **physical description** and is our focus in this chapter.

This is the part of cataloging that requires a lot of knowledge about the standard rules. It is the part of a cataloging class that frustrates the students, because there are so many rules and so many of them seem so silly and picky. In this chapter we will not be examining each one of these rules; to do so would required taking a full cataloging class. The hope, however, is to present to you a picture of basic physical description so that you can understand the information you arc sent by the vendors. One small warning before we begin: The rules discussed here are undergoing a big change. As catalogers focus on electronic information rather than printed books, they have found the need to reexamine the standardized rules that have been in use since the 1940s. Even the title of the rule book will be changing from *Anglo-American Cataloging Rules* (*AACR*) *to Resource Description and Access* (*RDA*). I have been following the progress of the changes in the rules and have come to the conclusion that even though the format of information is changing, the need to describe the item is that same and the rules will not affect the philosophy behind physical description; and so we push forward.

A LITTLE HISTORY ON CATALOGING RULES

Again we look to the end of the 1800s to find out why we have so many rules for physical description. The great thinkers of library science decided that it would be kind of nice if a person could go from one library to another, open up the catalog, and know exactly what type of information is given just based on the location of that information. Even a person who did not read English could go to the Library of Congress and know that the information on the first line of the catalog card would be (usually) the name of the author of the work. This is much like knowing that in any grocery store we go to, we will always find milk in the refrigerated section.

The men we have to thank for the rules that catalogers struggle with are Sir Anthony Panizzi of the British Museum in London, Charles Jewett of the Smithsonian Institute in Washington, D.C., and our good friend Charles A. Cutter. As with any great idea, these men did not work alone (there might have even been a few women working on the problem), but their ideas were the ones published, and therefore we credit them for the rules that formed the basis for the structure of the information we find on a catalog record. It was Cutter who said that a person should be able to find a book based on the author, title, and subject and that the library should be able to show what it has based on the author, subject, or type of literature. It was Jewett who proposed "stereotyped" cataloging so that libraries can share records and copy the cataloging of one library to another. In this way, he set the stage for the vendors we have today who will sell us our items with the cataloging already taken care of. If each library had its own way of cataloging, they could not offer this service.

In making these statements, the British and American library associations worked together to come up with rules for cataloging materials. Unable to come to complete agreement, the first international standards were published in two editions; one for the Americans and one for the British. The outbreak of World War II made further collaboration difficult; nevertheless, the American Library Association published its second edition of the national standards in 1941. The *Anglo-American Cataloguing Rules,* illustrating a true collaboration between the British and American library associations and later the Canadian Library Association, were published in 1967 and have since been updated regularly. Each time new rules are published, there are growing pains.

Catalogers complain that there are too many rules, or not enough rules, or that the needs of school and small libraries are being completely ignored. At the turn of the twenty-first century, cataloging committees came to the conclusion that changes in the delivery of information (from book to electronic formats) meant that the cataloging rules needed a complete reexamination. The new rules, to be called *Resource*

Description and Access, were scheduled to be published in 2009. However, at the time of writing this book, it is clear that a 2009 publication date may be a little optimistic and more research needs to be conducted before publishing new standards. It is an exciting time to be a cataloger!

For a nice, brief history of cataloging, take a look at the web site put together by the Joint Steering Committee for the Development of RDA: http://www.collectionscan ada.ca/jsc/history.html. It's helpful to keep in mind that these rules were constructed to make finding information easier for the library user even while we catalogers sit and struggle with them!

PHYSICAL DESCRIPTION

In the previous chapters we have focused on what catalogers call **intellectual description**, or describing what the item is about. In classifying an item we show the discipline or area of study that the item is most closely related to. In giving the item subject headings, we are also describing what the item is about. Physical description is simply that; a description of what the item is: the title, author, publisher, number of pages, length of playing time, and so on.

In looking at the physical description of an item, it will be helpful for us to start with an illustration and work our way around the information. However, before we look at the illustration, let us go back to our grocery clerk to see if she has found that "long curvy thing you peel before you eat the white part" for us. Turns out our description wasn't as good as we hoped it would be. She has provided us with two choices; one she calls a plantain, which is green; and the other she calls a banana, and it is yellow. It is the banana we are looking for, but because we neglected to say it was yellow, she brought us the two things that best matched our description. The lesson we learn here is that detail in physical description is very important. Now let's take a look at a catalog record as shown in Figure 3.1 that shows us a sample record and a model we can use for creating other records.

The column on the left side of Figure 3.1 shows what a catalog record might look like for the book with the title *The Rain in Spain* (this is a made up book used to illustrate the parts of the record). The column on the right side of the figure shows how to use the record as a model so that we can now catalog just about any book that comes to us. Let us take a closer look at the left column by putting it into a form that is typical of a card catalog or an online catalog as shown in Figure 3.2.

Most people who are new to the library profession have never seen the old card catalog with those 3" × 5" cards upon which the information about a book was typed (in the really old days, typed up by hand on a typewriter, and in the even older days, written out by hand after taking a class on penmanship for writing catalog cards!). The online catalogs most of us have today have held onto the "card" format for displaying information about the item. We will take a look at some online examples later in this chapter.

Sample	Model
Smith, Alex S. (Alex Simon)	Last name of author, First name (other information as needed)
The rain in Spain : agriculture in Spain / written by Alex S. Smith ; illustrated by Robin R. Rollins. – 5th ed. – New York : HarperCollins, c2006.	Title : subtitle / statement of responsibility ; other statement of responsibility. – Edition if there is one. – Place of publication : Publisher, copyright date or date of publication.
xii, 360 p. : ill. ; 24 cm. – (Agriculture around the world series)	Extent of item : illustrations; measurement of the item. – (Series statement if there is one)
Includes bibliographical references and index.	Note that there is a bibliography and index with the item.
CONTENTS: Effects of weather on agriculture – Effects of politics on agriculture – Effects of pollution on agriculture.	Note to show the chapter titles, or titles of volumes if there is more than one volume to a set.
SUMMARY: Explores the effects of weather, politics, and pollution on the agricultural industry in Spain.	Note to show the summary of the item.
ISBN: 0-07-012345-0 : $34.95	Numbers associated with the item, most often will be the ISBN
1. Agriculture – Spain. I. Rollins, Robin R. II. Title. III. Series	Tracings for the item.

Figure 3.1. A sample of a book catalog record and a template for a book record.

```
Smith, Alex S. (Alex Simon)                                    630.946
                                                               Sm511
                                                               2006

    The rain in Spain : agriculture in Spain / written by Alex S. Smith ; illustrated by

Robin R. Rollins. – 5ᵗʰ ed. – New York : HarperCollins, c2006.

    xii, 360 p. : ill. ; 24 cm. – (Agriculture around the world)


Includes bibliographical references and index.


CONTENTS: Effects of weather on agriculture – Effects of politics on agriculture –

Effects of pollution on agriculture.


SUMMARY: Explores the effects of weather, politics, and pollution on the agricultural

industry in Spain.


ISBN: 0-07-012345-0 : $34.95


1. Spain.  2. Agriculture – Spain.  I. Rollins, Robin  R.    II. Title.    III. Series.
```

Figure 3.2.   Sample catalog record for *The Rain in Spain.*

First, let's define what we see in Figure 3.2. In total, this information is referred to as a **catalog record** or **bibliographic record**, or record for short. It is a record because it is a written recording or account of the physical and intellectual content of the item. Librarians will often say, "What's on the record?" when asking about this information. So we'll call it a record too. Second, most of the information in the record must come from the item itself, and the title page for books is the most important source of information we have. Line by line, then, this is what we see:

- Smith, Alex S. (Alex Simon)
    - This line is called the main entry. Without getting into all of the theory of cataloging, suffice to say it's kind of a funny name for this line. It is very likely that this line will disappear with the new RDA standards. For now we'll think of it as the author line.
    - The name of the author is given with the last name first, then a comma, and then the first name as it is written on the title page.
    - Sometimes an author uses initials, but to make this author different from other authors with the same name, we need to add the full form of the name as we

see here in our example. Do not worry about this; if you receive a record like this, just accept it. If you have to catalog an item on your own and the author has an abbreviation in his or her name, simply accept it and don't try to find out what that initial stands for. It's included here so you don't get worried if you see it on your own records.

- This part of the record ends with a period unless there is a parenthesis, as is the case with our example.

- 630.946 Sm511 2006

    - This is the call number (the mix between the classification number [630.946], the Cutter number [Sm511], and the data of publication [2006]). It is usually located in the upper right-hand corner of the catalog record (sometimes it is on the upper left-hand corner, but for our examples we'll stick to the upper right-hand corner). It is not part of the physical description, but one would see it on the old cards and so it is here in our example. See chapter 1 for a reminder of how this number was created.

- The rain in Spain : agriculture in Spain / written by Alex S. Smith ; illustrated by Robin R. Rollins.

    - The next line is our "title and statement of responsibility."
    - Notice that in the title, only the first word "the" and the proper noun "Spain" are capitalized. When catalog cards were typed by hand, the rule makers tried to make the process as easy as possible, so not every word in the title is capitalized. This is sometimes confusing when we think back to writing bibliographies in school when our teachers told us to capitalize every word in the title. Just remember that in cataloging, capitalize only when you have to (first word, names of people and places, and the proper pronoun "I").
    - This title has two parts, called the title proper (The rain in Spain) and other title information (agriculture in Spain). The two parts are separated by a space, a colon (:), and another space.
    - The next part is the statement of responsibility. This means the person (or company) who is responsible for the content of the item. In books we ask who the author and illustrator are. In other items we might ask who is the performing group or who drew the map or who created the sculpture. Movie makers are a whole different problem that we will discuss later in the chapter.
    - Notice that the title ends with a space, a slash (/) and a space because we have a statement of responsibility. If there was no statement of responsibility, as might be the case with a movie, then there would just be a period (.).
    - In our example we have an author (Alex S. Smith) and an illustrator (Robin R. Rollins). These two have two different jobs and so are separated by a space, a semicolon (;), and a space. If there were two authors, because they have the same job (writing) there would be a comma between the two names like this: Alex S. Smith, Tom Jones (if there is no "and" on the title page) or Alex S. Smith and Tom Jones (if there is an "and" on the title page).

- Notice that in the statement of responsibility we write the names as they appear on the title page (Alex S. Smith) and not as we have written on the first line: Smith, Alex S. (Alex Simon). This is because the title and statement of responsibility are written down according to how they appear on the title page. If we wrote according to the authority (Alex Simon) or in reverse order (Smith, Alex S.) then it would look strange to the library user and would be confusing.

- In this section we've stated that the information is recorded as it appears on the title page, or the part of the item that has the most information about it (for example, the title screen on a computer program or web site). Catalogers call this the **chief source of information**. The exception is for funny lettering or intentional misspellings. For example, the poet, E. E. Cummings always published with his name in lower-case letters (e. e. cummings), but in the statement of responsibility, the name would be capitalized. Children's books are famous for playing with words in the title; for example, Barbara Robinson's book, *The Best School Year Ever,* where on the title page "worst" is crossed out and "best" is written over it. What is the title? According to the Library of Congress, the title is *The Best School Year Ever.* According to the publisher's web site (http://www2.scholastic. com/browse/book.jsp?id=690), the title is *The Worst Best School Year Ever.* Appendix C shows us how to deal with these kinds of "mistakes," but for now we should follow the rule that we record this information as it appears on the chief source of information.

- —5th ed.

  - This next area is for any statement of edition of the item.
  - In our example we see this is the fifth edition of the book.
  - Notice that we use the number "5" instead of writing out fifth; we also abbreviate edition to "ed."
  - This area is either on a new line or has the double dash in front of it and ends in a period.
  - If the item you are cataloging does not have an edition statement then there is no information about an edition on the catalog record; it's okay to not have an edition statement.
  - If the information is not on the front of the title page, check the back of the title page; edition statements are often found there.

- —New York : HarperCollins, c2006.

  - This is the publication information line.
  - As with the edition statement, it is either a new line or has the double dash in front of it.
  - When cataloging books, the information for this line can come from the title page or the back of the title page.
  - This line always ends with a period.

- Sometimes there will be more than one place of publication. If this happens and you are creating your own catalog record, write down the name of the place that is in the United States or that is written in the biggest letters on the title page if there is no place in the United States given. Don't panic if you see more than one place named on your catalog record. There are lots of rules to explain this, but for our needs, we'll list only one place of publication.
- Notice that the date has a "c" in front of it like this: c2006. This means that we have a copyright date instead of a date of publication. These days we usually see copyright dates in books, so most records will have that little "c." Don't panic if you don't see the "c," because a date of publication is as good as a copyright date. You'll know the type of date you have if you are doing your own cataloging, because the date (most often found on the back of the title page) will have the copyright symbol (©) or will have the word copyright in front of the date. If all you see is a date, then take this as a publication date and don't include the "c."
- You might also see two dates, like this: 2004, c2003. This is more common in older items but can still be seen today, so we mention it here. Don't worry about having both a publication and copyright date. If you are cataloging something and you are not sure what to do, you can record just the copyright date; that's a legal move to make.
- This information ends with a period.

- xii, 360 p. : ill. ; 24 cm.

  - This is the physical extent of the item. For books it records the number of pages, any illustrations included in the item, and the size of the book.
  - In our example, this line begins with "xii." These are the page numbers in Roman numerals. Some books begin with preliminary pages before the real text begins. If you see a number of x (10) or higher, you need to record it. If there are fewer than 10 preliminary pages then you can ignore the roman numerals. Don't panic if your record doesn't have Roman numerals before the other numbers; not every book has them. If your book begins with Roman numerals and then the next Arabic number follows in sequence then you don't record the Roman numerals. For example, the last Roman numeral is "xi" and the next page is numbered "12" then just record the last page number in the book and you're done.
  - The page numbers are followed by a note of illustrations if there are any in the book or by the measurement of the book. In the old days, one would have to record exactly what type of illustrations were in a book: color photographs, maps, forms, or whatever. Today, all we have to add is "ill." and we're done. Lucky us!
  - If there are no illustrations, go right to the semicolon (;) and enter the height of the book. Books are measured in centimeters and to the next highest centimeter at that. So a book that measures 29.3 centimeters would be recorded as 30 centimeters. Folks who argue about making cataloging easier often say that

no one cares how tall a book is. That is a matter of opinion. For now, we'll record that information.

- This part ends in a period.
- For items that are not books; we list the extent of the item, the timing if available, the format, and the dimensions. Like so:
  - 1 sound disc (ca. 30 min.) ; stereo : 4 3/4 in.
  - What we have here is a sound disc, probably a CD, that runs for 30 minutes, has been recorded in stereo sound, and measures four inches in diameter.
  - We could also record the first part as "1 CD-ROM" if we wanted to be nice to our users, although when catalogers first started cataloging these things they did not use the general term "CD-ROM" so you could see it both ways in your catalog. "CD-ROM" is a rather antiquated term today but it is still the official term used by librarians so we need to use it too.
  - 1 DVD (120 min.) ; col, stereo : 4 3/4 in.
  - What we have here is what catalogers call a laser optical disc, but to our users it is a DVD, and we have permission to call it just that.
  - It has a running time of two hours, which we have recorded here in minutes, 120 of them. The movie is in color with a stereo soundtrack and has the standard measure of a disc, 4 3/4 inches in diameter.

- —(Agriculture around the world)

  - If a book is part of a series, then this is the place we write down that information.
  - Like our other lines, this information is a new line or has the double dashes in front of it.
  - Like the title statement, only the first word of the series is capitalized.
  - Series titles are always in parentheses, and there is no period at the end of this line.
  - Notice that there is nothing here that tells us this is a series title except that it is in parentheses and we now know that when we see information like that on the record that it is a series title. How do our users know this is a series title? In the card environment, they have to be educated about that. If we have to enter this information, the item will usually be designed such that it is clear to us that this is a series title.
  - If there is no series title, then don't worry about creating one.
  - For online systems, this information is usually noted as series title information, so having an online system can really be a benefit to our users.

- Includes bibliographical references and index.

  - This line starts what catalogers call the "notes" section. In this section we don't get the information from the chief source of information but from what we see in looking at the item itself. It should be noted here that the notes section is not limited to what we see in our example. We can also add here notes about the creators and performers in the case of movies, sound recordings, and computer software.

- This line tells us that the book has an index and "bibliographical references." The references could be in the form of footnotes at the bottom of the pages of the book or in a separate reference section.
- Sometimes it seems silly to record so much information, but it can be important. For example, for a student working on a research project, knowing that the book has an index means that he won't have to read the entire book to see if it has what he's looking for. Another user may want to know that the book has a reference section so she can do more reading on the subject based on what the author of the item has quoted in the book.
- Index and bibliography information can be recorded on two separate lines or one line together.
- This information is always on a new line and always ends with a period.
- The notes area is also used to record other types of information. Maybe the item is missing pages. Maybe the item is signed by the author. Maybe the item was written by one of the library staff members. Things like this are all recorded in this area. Each note has its own line.

- CONTENTS: Effects of weather on agriculture — Effects of politics on agriculture — Effects of pollution on agriculture.

  - The information here includes chapter, volume, or section titles of an item.
  - This line always begins with "CONTENTS," always written in all capital letters, and always ends in a period.
  - For books, this information may be individual chapter titles or may be the titles of volumes. For example, let's say you have *A History of US* by Joy Hakim. You might have a note in your record that looks like this: CONTENTS: Bk. 1. The first Americans — bk. 2. Making thirteen colonies — bk. 3. From colonies to country — bk. 4. The new nation — bk. 5. Liberty for all? — bk. 6. War, terrible war — bk. 7. Reconstruction and reform — bk. 8. An age of extremes — bk. 9. War, peace, and all that jazz — bk. 10. All the people — bk. 11. Sourcebook and index. We do this because we want only one catalog record for the item but we want to show our patrons what is included in this multi-volume set.
  - For items that are not books, this area may include the names of the songs or the different computer programs on the disc or the different playing options on a DVD.
  - Whatever kind of information is being recorded, the sections are separated by a space, a double dash (—), and a space.

- SUMMARY: Explores the effects of weather, politics, and pollution on the agricultural industry in Spain.

  - This is a short, usually one sentence, statement that gives the user an idea of what the item is about. In the 1990s the Library of Congress announced that it no longer had the resources to include summary statements for works of fiction.

The library world went nuts, especially those who worked with children and young adults for whom summary statements are so vitally important for helping with recommending books to read. Summary statements are still included in new works, but you might get used to creating your own statements because you never know what will happen in the future.

- There is no set format for the summary statement except that it ends with a period.
- Creating a summary statement is an extreme effort of creative writing to provide a general sense of the item without giving away the ending.
- You should feel free to adapt the summary statements that are provided by your vendor. Sometimes the statements do not accurately represent what the item is about. So if you get an item with a summary statement that doesn't really satisfy you, feel free to add to it or even rewrite it completely.

- ISBN: 0-07-012345-0 : $34.95

  - This part of the record records numbers that are connected to the item.
  - For books, this is the ISBN; but for magazines this would be the ISSN.
  - You will recognize this number on the item because it will have the abbreviation (ISBN, ISSN) on the item itself; you will not need to make up this number.
  - Other items, such as sound and film records, carry with them their own standard numbers. It will be clear from the item what the standard number is. Simply record the number as it appears on the item.
  - Notice that our note includes the price of the item. It is common practice to include this as part of the record, but we may not want our users to see this out in the open. Other ways may be used for keeping track of the cost of the item (to be described in the next chapter), and you should feel free to delete this information if it is provided here by your vendor.
  - One reason we may not want this information showing is if it is an inexpensive item, we could have a user who thinks it's all right to keep the item and simply pay the small amount with the thought that we would take that money and replace the item. Of course that's not usually what happens when an item is lost. Often this money goes into a fund that we may not even have control over, and at any rate the money may be used to buy something else and then that lost item is not replaced. If you have a policy of a flat "lost fee" and that fee is more or less than the printed cost of the item, you could run into problems with your users in paying a fine that does not reflect the "true" cost of the item. The point is that this information is often best recorded in a less public part of the catalog record.

- 1. Spain. 2. Agriculture—Spain.

  - This part of the record is called the **tracing** part. Tracings help the user find the item in alternative ways besides our "main entry" (author) or the title. We "trace" for subject headings, other title information, other people responsible for the content of the item (like an illustrator), or series title.

- In this part we see something that we recognize as the subject heading.
- Our example shows two subject headings for this title. As discussed in the previous chapter, there is no limit to the number of subject headings we can give to an item although most often we don't see more than three to five subject headings.
- Subject headings are numbered using Arabic numbers (1, 2, 3, and so on).
- As we learned in the previous chapter, subject headings are not part of physical description; however, they are a prominent part of the catalog record and so are presented in the figure and discussed here.

- I. Rollins, Robin. R. II. Title. III. Series.

  - Here we see the tracings for other title information and for series title.
  - Our example includes another author (or an illustrator in our case) so that name also appears here.
  - Each tracing here is listed using Roman numerals (I, II, III, and so on).

Let's take another look at our sample catalog record with each part of the record labeled for us as given in Figure 3.3.

If your library purchases catalog cards, the above figures illustrate how the cataloging information is presented for the users. But if you have a computer based or automated system, the information, while it remains the same, may be presented in a slightly different format. When companies first started developing automated cataloging systems, the information was formatted to look just like the catalog card. It was comforting to both librarians and users to see the information in the way they were used to seeing it being presented. However, as systems became more and more sophisticated it became clear that users didn't need information presented in a "librarian" kind of way. Similarly, librarians also found that they no longer needed to see information presented like a catalog card. After all they had tossed the card catalog, so why bother with trying to recreate it on the computer? The result is that the same information we just discussed is now presented in a much clearer format even though this does not change the type of information we need for cataloging. Let's take a look at what a typical computer screen might look like for *The Rain in Spain* as presented in Figure 3.4.

This record is so much easier to understand! We don't have to guess what that thing is in parentheses; it tells us it's the series title. In fact we don't even have to bother with the parentheses! The advantage of online databases these days is that often they have links in the record. So if users want to know everything the library has under the series title "Agriculture around the world," they just click on that link and up comes all the other titles in the series. Likewise, if they want to know what the library has that was illustrated by Rollins, they click on Rollins's name and up comes all of the records that have traced Rollins as being responsible for the illustrations of other works. In

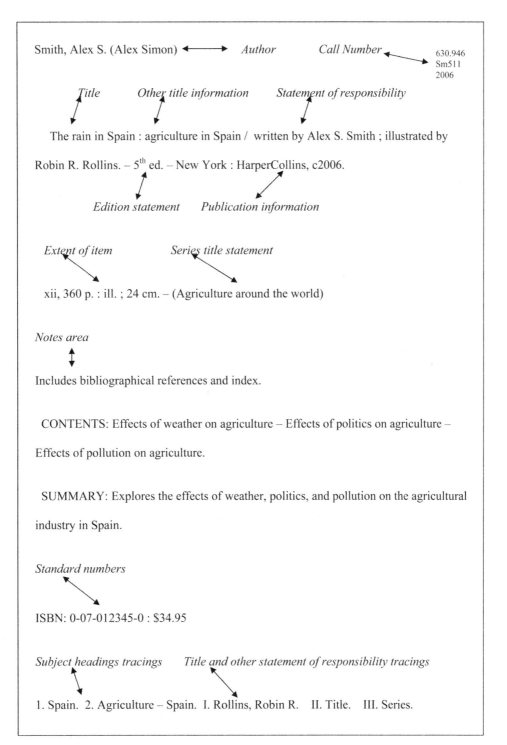

Figure 3.3. **Sample record of *The Rain in Spain* with cataloging labels.**

Call Number:	630.946 Sm511 2006
Author:	Smith, Alex S. (Alex Simon)
Title:	The rain in Spain : agriculture in Spain
Edition:	5th ed.
Publisher:	New York : HarperCollins
Date:	2006.
Description:	xii, 360 p. : ill. ; 24 cm.
Series title:	Agriculture around the world
Notes:	Includes bibliographical references and index.
Contents:	Effects of weather on agriculture – Effects of politics on agriculture – Effects of pollution on agriculture.
Summary:	Explores the effects of weather, politics, and pollution on the agricultural industry in Spain.
ISBN:	0-07-012345-0 : $34.95
Subjects:	Spain.
	Agriculture – Spain.
Related names:	Rollins, Robin R., ill.

Figure 3.4.   Sample online catalog record for *The Rain in Spain*.

fact, in some systems, the names of the author(s) or illustrator(s) are listed in direct form (first name first), which makes it even that much easier to read! As librarians, we have to understand how the record works, but our users do not; and that's a good thing for them! While this type of display is infinitely clearer to our users, not every system displays the information like this, so both the traditional (Figure 3.2) and newer (Figure 3.4) samples are shown here.

Non-Book Materials

Items such as DVDs, web sites, and audiobooks are described using the same *AACR* rules as we have already discussed for books. The difference comes in accounting for aspects of these items such as performers, related sites, and playing times that simply are not part of book items. In this section we will take a very brief look at physical description for non-book items, recalling that the format of the record remains the same regardless of the type of item being cataloged.

In cataloging books, it is pretty clear who is responsible for the intellectual content of the item. Usually there is a clear author (or authors) and illustrator (or illustrators). Sometimes we have a book that has been edited by one or more people, and that presents a little bit of a problem for us. Typically you can expect that the editor will not get that main entry. In other words, the editor ends up in the "related authors" line of the catalog record instead of the "author" line because he or she did not actually write the content of the book but brought other people together to write the content. Likewise, if we think about the people involved in putting together non-book materials—the producer, the director, the performers, the script writers, the program developers, and on and on—one must wonder who is most responsible to warrant that main entry line. Since it is difficult to assign main responsibility with non-book materials, we opt to use the title of the item as the main entry rather than a person. Then we make tracings for the names of the people involved with putting the whole thing together.

Recording Material Type

In the title line, we will insert the type of material it is that we are cataloging after the main part of the title. Figure 3.5 shows us examples of titles and the types of words used to define the material type.

These examples have lots of things to notice about them. In all of these examples, the name of the type of material is included in brackets, [ ], to show that we, the catalogers, added that to the title and it did not come from the item itself. Now let's look at each example separately.

Looking at example number 1, Holes [videorecording] or Holes [VHS], we notice that videotapes are called "videorecording" by *AACR*. Who in your library looks for a videorecording? We do not know. But happily the cataloging rule makers recently agreed that our users don't really understand what a "videorecording" is and so decided

1.   The movie *Holes* in video format:

Holes [videorecording]

Or

Holes [VHS]

2. The movie *Holes* in DVD format:

Holes [videorecording]

Or

Holes [DVD]

3.   The music recording *You're Beautiful* on a CD-ROM:

You're beautiful [sound recording]

Or

You're beautiful [CD-ROM]

Figure 3.5.   Titles and material types.
(Continued)

that to use the vernacular term, the term we all use in every day language, is acceptable cataloging practice. That accounts for our second option of using "[VHS]" to note the type of material. However, it is not very common to see the "VHS" notation for video-tapes. Perhaps this is because the videotape is a very old technology and catalogers are used to using "videorecording." If you think your users would be happier seeing "VHS" the rules allow you to do this, but don't expect to see it in cataloging that you buy.

Example number 2, Holes [videorecording] or Holes [DVD], is very similar to example number 1 and also gives us two ways to describe an item in DVD format. Notice that our first option is the same as our videotape; that is "videorecording." Also, like our first example, we can use the common term, in this case "DVD," in that format spot. Unlike our videotape example, it is becoming more common to see the DVD designation than the videorecording designation. But, in looking at cataloging that you have bought for a DVD item, it is just as likely that you will still see "videorecording."

4. The audio book *The Dangerous Book for Boys* on tape cassette

The dangerous book for boys [sound recording]

5.　　Audio book *The Dangerous Book for Boys* on CD-ROM

The dangerous book for boys [sound recording]

Or

The dangerous book for boys [CD-ROM]

6. Audio book *The Dangerous Book for Boys* as MP3 file

The dangerous book for boys [sound recording]

Or

The dangerous book for boys [MP3]

Figure 3.5.　(*Continued*)

Again, you have the freedom to use "[DVD]" instead of "[videorecording]" for this type of material, and you should know that both terms are used for this type of material.

Examples number 3–6 are all examples of sound recordings. This term, "sound recording," is used to note an item that is just recorded sound without any pictures or images. Of course we all know that these days, MP3 and CDs may very well have images in the files but for the most part, these types of files are used for sound, at least according to our cataloging rule makers. So if you have a pile of items that include tape cassettes, CDs, MP3 files, or any other type of recorded sound, using the broad phrase "sound recording" will cover all of those item types. If you have a large collection of CDs, or if you have a user population that would be best served with more specific designations, then by all means, use the second options in each of these examples to make a separation between your tapes, CDs, and other types of recordings.

Recording Physical Description

When cataloging books, we create a line in the catalog record that tells us how many pages the book has, if it has illustrations, and how big it is. In non-book materials, we do something similar. We record how many of the items we have in the set and how long it runs, how it has been recorded, and what size it is. So for a CD recording of *Harry Potter and the Deathly Hallows,* we would say: 17 sound discs (21 hr., 39 min.) : digital ; 4 3/4 in. Which, translated into English, means we have 17 discs that play for almost 22 hours and have been digitally recorded, and each disc is 4 and 3/4 inches. Remember, in this part of the record, we depend on the item itself. We will have in front of us all of those discs, and somewhere on the box it will tell us what the running time is and that they have all been digitally recorded. For size, we use the diameter of the disc, which for standard-size discs is always 4 3/4 inches.

Let's say we have the set of videotapes for the Ken Burns production of *Jazz.* The set has 10 cassettes that run a total of almost 19 hours, the show was in color and of course had sound (after all it was about music!), and it came with a book that listed each part of the show in an index form. This book is 95 pages, has illustrations, and measures 22 centimeters high. Give this some thought before looking at the next line that shows what this would look like. . .

Here is the answer:

10 videocassettes (ca. 19 hrs.) : sd., col. ; 1/2 in. + 1 index (95 p. : ill. ; 22 cm.)

What you should notice right away is that the information about the index looks just like the information on the line for a book we described earlier in this chapter. Other than that, this looks pretty much like our first example. As with our previous example, the line begins with the number of tapes in the set (10) just like we start a book description with the number of pages in the book. This is followed by the running time, always recorded in parentheses. This information is usually on the item itself (in this case on each tape) or on the box. The "ca." means that this is an approximate running time. What we didn't have in the first example was the "sd., col." information. This is cataloging shorthand for sound (sd.) and color (col.). In sound recordings we don't have to say the item has sound because that's what it is. Color refers to whether the images are in color or black and white only (which would be recorded as b&w). In our example, the program includes some black and white images but the overall production of the program is in color and we note it as such. So for sound recordings we make note of how the sound was recorded, and in videorecordings we make a note if there is sound and the color of the images. Finally we have the designation of the size of the tapes. A long time ago there were two types of tapes; vhs tapes were ½" size and beta tapes were ¾" size. Today the beta tapes are gone, but we still record the size of the vhs tapes. Let's look again at the physical description line and review each part of it as shown in Figure 3.6.

In thinking about the rest of the cataloging record for non-book materials, there are not too many other differences except in the area of notes. Four different kinds of notes are described here that are specific to non-book items: material type, responsibility, origin of title, and user warnings. Figure 3.7 shows examples of notes for different kinds of items.

In the catalog record, we don't need to say in the notes area that we have a book, because it is assumed that the item is a book. But with non-book items, we do want to

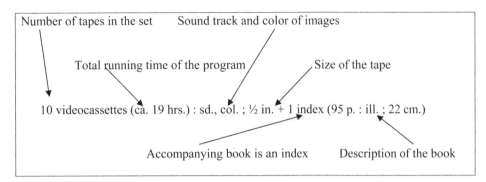

Figure 3.6.   Physical description for videotapes.

define for our users that they are looking at a record of an item that is not a book. So we make a quick note and hope the readers will look at that part of the record. Here is where we can use common terms to show that we have a VHS item, a DVD item, a web page, or a computer program. As of the date of this publication, there has been no official ruling on how to describe blu-ray DVDs. You are probably safe in assuming that you can make the note, "Blu-ray DVD" but that is an unofficial assumption.

When cataloging books, there is almost always a title page that, we remember, we use as the chief source of information for the title of the book. But in non-book materials there are a number of places from which we can get a title, from the box cover to the title screen to a specific web site. For non-book items, you need to supply a note that explains where the title came from. See Figure 3.7 for examples.

Because it is often difficult to define a main author for a non-book item, the notes area is used to record the names of people important to the content of the item. This can be the film producer, director, the actors or performers, the software designers, or other important people. If you think someone is important, here is where you would record that data. One thing to remember is that if you want your library users to find an item based on a person's name, you have to make a tracing for it. We'll see in the next chapter how to do that.

One other different note would be a rating or age-use note. This is especially true for movies and computer software. It is not a required part of the catalog record, but we know our users would be very happy to see on the record some information about the appropriateness of the use of the item. Is it just for adults or perhaps only little kids would be interested in it. Use the notes area to describe the age level for this item.

CONCLUSION

Now that we know the type of information to be included in a catalog record, we need to know how it gets into the database. Most of the time, you will be buying the catalog records when you buy your items, or if you are part of a larger library system,

- Material type:

    o Notes: VHS.

    o Notes: DVD.

    o Notes: Web page.

    o Notes: CD-ROM.

- Origin of title:

    o Notes: Title taken from main web page.

    o Notes: Title taken from container cover.

- Content responsibility:

    o Notes: Directed by Ken Burns; written by Geoffrey C. Ward; produced by Ken Burns and Lynn Novick.

    o Notes: Performers, Paul McCartney, John Lennon, George Harrison, Ringo Starr.

    o Notes: Narrator, Jim Dale.

    o Notes: Cast: Hilary Swank, Clint Eastwood, Morgan Freeman

    o Notes: Cast: Hilary Swank (Maggie Fitzgerald), Clint Eastwood (Frankie Dunn), Morgan Freeman (Eddie Scrap-Iron Dupris).

- Appropriate audience:

    o Notes: "Content rated by ESRB: Teen, animated violence, realistic violence."–Container.

    o Notes: MPAA rating: PG-13; for violence.

    o Notes: "For all audiences" – Inside booklet.

Figure 3.7.   Sample notes for non-book items.

you have a central office that does all of the cataloging. But what happens if you have to fix a record (maybe the title was misspelled) or if you want to add a subject heading or if someone donates an item to your library and you want to add it to your catalog? In the next chapter we will explore the means by which we will get the information from the item to the catalog record by following the rules for intellectual and physical description.

Points to Remember about Chapter 3

- Physical description is the practice of describing what the item is like rather than the topics covered or the discipline to which it belongs.
- Rules for describing an item are covered in *Anglo-American Cataloging Rules.*
- Things that are part of the physical description are:
  - Name of the person or people responsible for the content of the item
  - The title of the item and any other title information that is part of the item
  - The name of the publisher and date of publication
  - The extent of the item (number of pages, type of illustrations, running time, etc.)
  - Name of the series of the item if necessary
  - Standard numbers associated with the item
  - Special notes about the item (autographs, missing pages, etc.)
- Non-book materials follow the same rules as book materials with some changes to account for information that is not found in book items.
- The physical description and the intellectual description put together make up the catalog record.

PROBLEM SET

1. If your author is Susan B. Baron, how would you write that in the author (main entry) line?

2. Write this information in your title and statement of responsibility line (hint: watch for capitalization in the title):

   The rights of humans
   A story about civil rights in the united states
   By George Smith and Gale Robbins
   Illustrated by John Adams

3. What kind of physical description line would you write if you had a set of 12 cassette tapes that run about 14 hours and are digitally recorded with a book that has 25 pages, pictures, and measures 24 centimeters?

ANSWERS

1. Not knowing what the "B" stands for in Susan's name, we simply write her name like so:

   Baron, Susan B. Remember that in the main entry form, we write last name first and then first name and any initials that follow.

2. The problem is a little bit tricky in terms of capitalization but otherwise is straightforward and will look like this:

The rights of humans : a story about civil rights in the United States / by George Smith and Gale Robbins ; illustrated by John Adams.

Here we have to be careful that our proper noun (United States) is capitalized even if not capitalized in the title and that the designations of the authors and illustrator are not capitalized.

3. This is a common problem in dealing with non-book and book items together as one item. If you don't forget the common structure for physical description, you should be all right:

12 sound cassettes (ca. 14 hours) : digital + 1 book (25 p. : ill. ; 24 cm.)

Unless the tapes are of an unusual size, you don't need to mention the dimensions of the cassette tape case.

CHAPTER 4

What You Need to Know about MARC and Automated Systems

MARC, or more correctly MARC21, is a child of the 1960s. It developed with the birth of computer use in business but did not become a part of the common vocabulary of librarians until the mid- to late 1970s. It is important to understand that MARC is the format used to get information from the item to the computer database. MARC is not a cataloging standard. We've already learned about cataloging standards in chapter 3.

When cataloging moved from the card to the computer, librarians needed to create a language to speak to the computer. That language is **MAchine Readable Cataloging**, or **MARC**. In chapter 3 we learned that cataloging standards in the United States are in the form of *AACR*. We learned about the standards, but we did not go over each individual rule. Likewise, in this chapter we will learn about some parts of the computer program but we will not learn about every detail. A good resource to have when thinking about the catalog record or cataloging your own materials is a file from the Library of Congress; Understanding MARC Bibliographic: Machine Readable Cataloging (available at: http://www.loc.gov/marc/umb/). We are going to review the MARC record using a program that is available to us on the Internet. That program is called OPALS (Open-source Automated Library System) and is available at this site: http://www.opals-na.org/. Open source programs are becoming very popular these days. They are programs based on the idea that all software should be accessible and open to public use. One caveat about open source software: Open source does not mean free. Sometimes the software is free; sometimes there is a cost. We'll talk later in chapter 6 about other systems for creating library databases.

MARC FORMAT

Let us take another look at a catalog record from chapter 3 for our made-up book: *The Rain in Spain* (see Figure 4.1).

What we have to do with this information is put it into our computer. In real life, we would not be taking this information from a card, but from the item itself. We are "translating" the card information to the computer here, just for the sake of illustrating the process. When we make this translation, the information will appear as our example in Figure 4.2.

This record can look a bit intimidating, but looking at it closely, you will see the familiar information we had in our "card" format of the record. The difference here is

---

Smith, Alex S. (Alex Simon)   630.946
                                                                 Sm511
                                                                 2006

The rain in Spain : agriculture in Spain / written by Alex S. Smith ; illustrated by

Robin R. Rollins. – 5th ed. – New York : HarperCollins, c2006.

Xii, 360 p. : ill. ; 24 cm. – (Agriculture around the world series)

Includes bibliographical references and index.

CONTENTS: Effects of weather on agriculture – Effects of politics on agriculture –

Effects of pollution on agriculture.

SUMMARY: Explores the effects of weather, politics, and pollution on the agricultural

industry in Spain.

ISBN: 0-07-012345-0 : $34.95

1. Agriculture – Spain. I. Rollins, Robin R. II. Title. III. Series

---

Figure 4.1.   Catalog record for *The Rain in Spain*.

```
020 # # a 0070123450
        c $34.95
082 1 4 a 630.946 Sm511 2006
        2 14
100 1 # a Smith, Alex S.
        q Alex Simon
245 1 4 a The rain in Spain :
        b agriculture in Spain /
        c written by Alex S. Smith ; illustrated by Robin R. Rollins.
260 # # a New York :
        b HarperCollins,
        c 2006.
300 # # a xii, 360 p. :
        b ill. ;
        c 24 cm.
440 # 0 a Agriculture around the world series
504 # # a Includes bibliographic references and index.
505 0 # a Effects of weather on agriculture – Effects of politics on agriculture – Effects of
pollution on agriculture.
520 # # a Explores the effects of weather, politics, and pollution on the agricultural
industry in Spain.
650 # # a Agriculture
        z Spain.
700 1 # a Rollins, Robin R.
        e ill.
```

Figure 4.2. The MARC record for *The Rain in Spain*.

the computer information. Computers are not smart, so we have to tell them what to do every step of the way. Each numbered line in this record is called a **tag** or **field**. Those words, although technically not the same, are used to refer to the same thing. Catalogers might ask, "What's in the 100 tag?" or, "What's in the 020 field?" and they mean the same thing; that is, "Tell me what is in the 100 or 020 line." Look to see where the title of our book is located in Figure 4.2. Now let's look at it close up as shown in Figure 4.3.

What we see in Figure 4.3 is information that looks almost familiar. We can pick out the title, but we also see things that are unfamiliar to us. First, look at the beginning of the line: "**245**." That is the number of the tag or field. Catalogers will say, "What's in the 245 field?" Which means, "What is the title and statement of responsibility area of the record?" Notice that each part of this area is on a new line and that each line is preceded by a letter, in this case "a," "b," or "c." These letters mark the **subfields** of the 245 field. Looking back at Figure 4.2, we see that not every part of every numbered line follows an a, b, c format (see, for example, the field numbered 650). We also see that some lines only have one letter (see, for example, the field numbered 520). Other than those numbers and letters, the information should look familiar to you.

The one other part of the line to look at is the information between the number "245" and the subfield "a." Looking down the record in Figure 4.2, we see numbers and number signs. The two numbers together are called **indicators**, and they are

```
245 1 4 a The rain in Spain :
        b agriculture in Spain /
        c written by Alex S. Smith ; illustrated by Robin R. Rollins.
```

Figure 4.3.   The 245 field, or title and statement of responsibility line, for
The Rain in Spain, **in MARC format.**

instructions to the computer on what to do with the information that is about to be presented. So, in the 245 field, the indicator 14 (pronounced one four, not fourteen) tells the computer that there is an author for this item (or 100 field) and that when the computer is looking for this item, it should look under the word "rain" and not the word "the." You see, in the old days, when librarians typed their own cards and filed the cards in the card catalog themselves, they knew when there was author information on the card and they had learned to ignore the initial articles (the, a, an) and file under the next word; in our case the card would be filed under the letter "r" for "rain." The second indicator (in this case, the 4) says to the computer, skip the first four spaces in the subfield "a" line (that's t-h-e-space) and file this record under the letter "r." Initial articles (the, a, an) are skipped when filing cards, so we have to tell the computers to skip them when filing the electronic records. The second indicator for a title starting with the initial article "a" would be 2 (one for the letter "a" and one for the space after it). The second indicator for a title starting with the initial article "an" would be 3 (one for the letter "a," one for the letter "n," and one for the space after it). Remember that computers are rather stupid. Where humans are smart and can recognize information, computers have to be told everything; they do not think for themselves. This means that one has to be really careful in creating a catalog record. If you have a title that begins with the word "the" and you forget to put that 4 in the second indicator place in the 245 field, the computer will look for this item under the letter "t" for "the" and the item will never be found by the user. Ignoring that second indicator in the 245 field is probably the most common mistake new catalogers make in creating MARC records. One more note about these indicators; notice that in the record shown in Figure 4.2, some indicators are numbers and others are number signs (#). The number sign (#) is used in the OPALS program to tell us that this indicator is blank. In library talk, we say the indicator is undefined; the word "blank" will work for us. Not every indicator space has a purpose, and so we leave it blank. In some programs you will see the number sign as shown here, but others will use the underscore (_) sign and still others will just have a blank space. What is important here is that you recognize an undefined indicator when you see one. More importantly, what you need to know is that in most programs you will not need to bother with the indicators except in the case of that second indicator in the 245 field, which is why we've spent so much time describing it here.

Because we have been reading about cataloging, looking at the rest of Figure 4.2, we can make sense of most of the other information. Of course our users have not read any books about cataloging, and so if they saw what we see in this figure they might never come back to our library! So automated programs developed what we call a **public display** so our users do not have to see the record with all of those numbers and such. The public display takes the information from the MARC record and puts it into a form that our users can (we hope) understand. Figure 4.4 shows an example of the public display for our book.

Each type of automated system is a little different in how it shows the public the catalog record. Some show the book covers, some link to reviews about the items, and still others have links to web sites. We show this catalog record to illustrate the difference between what the cataloger sees and what the user sees.

The MARC format was created by the librarians who worked in the Library of Congress for in-house use. That means they never meant for every cataloger in the world to use the system they were developing. But, as we saw with the *Library of Congress Subject Headings*, the power of the Library of Congress is very strong, and soon librarians were asking for access to this MARC program. Commercial vendors piggybacked on the work of the Library of Congress, and soon anyone with enough money could buy a program that was based on MARC for their own libraries. The structure of MARC is not self-explanatory. Looking at a plain MARC record with no information in it can be a little scary. Figure 4.5 shows us what an "empty" MARC record looks like. Comparing Figure 4.2 with Figure 4.5, we see information that we recognize, but in Figure 4.5 we have identified the meaning of each field. This might look a little scary at first, but there is little information here that we haven't already learned.

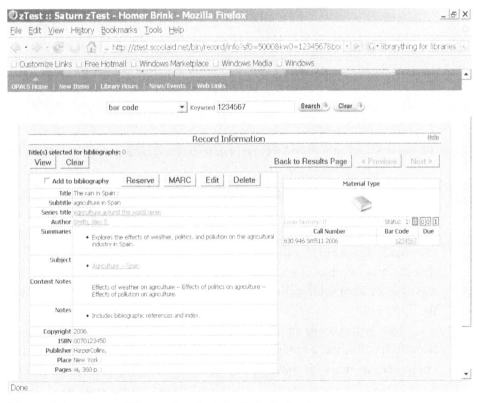

Figure 4.4.   The public display for *The Rain in Spain*.

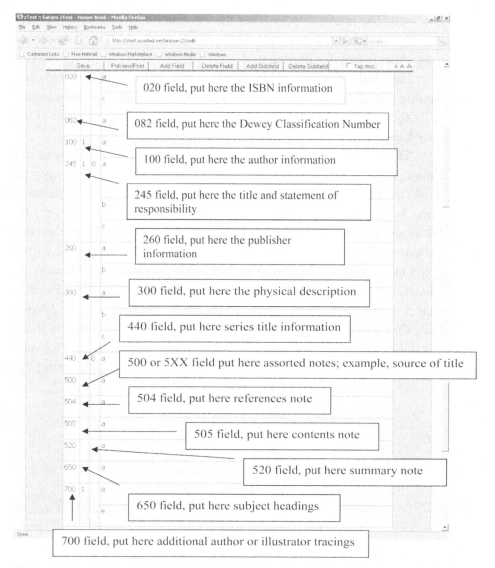

Figure 4.5.   "Empty" MARC record. Reprinted with permission from OPALS.

Most programs, either open source or commercial based, will also provide some way for the cataloger to know what goes in each field without having to memorize all of the field rules. Figure 4.6 shows an example of part of an empty record with this information provided by the program. Notice that this MARC record is for a DVD and that the program has already supplied for you the special things you need to have for this type of item such as the dimensions of the item in field 300 and the subfield h in the 245 field.

This brings us to another point about the MARC record. Nearly everything you need to have in the catalog record has its own subfield. Remember our rather dumb computer; we have to make it pay attention to each part of the catalog record. We have to say, "Hey, computer! New information coming your way!" To do this, we use the subfields. Let's look again at the 245 fields in both Figure 4.5 and Figure 4.6. In

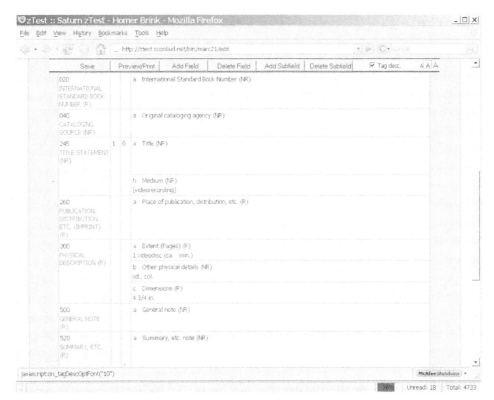

Figure 4.6. Empty MARC record with helpful information. Reprinted with permission from OPALS.

Figure 4.5 we have a 245 field for the title and statement of responsibility of a book. It has three subfields—a, b, and c—that tell us here is the title (subfield a), here is the other title information (subfield b), and here is the statement of responsibility (subfield c). In Figure 4.6 we have only two subfields in the 245 field (a and h). We know that the subfield a means this is the title. Now we ask, "What happened to subfields b and c, and what in the world is subfield h!?" Remember that in discussing other media in chapter 3, we said that media will almost never have a statement of responsibility; so out goes subfield c. It is not necessarily the case that media will not have subtitles, but more often than not they don't, and so out goes subfield b. Remember too that we said that in cataloging media we have to say what it is and we put this information in brackets after the title. Our computer program has automatically provided us a space to put that information, and in fact has already provided the information itself in the subfield h like this: "[videorecording]." We're so lucky that we don't have to worry about it. Now we can change it to DVD if we want to as described in chapter 3 or we can leave it like it is and not worry about typing in that information ourselves. We hope that using a computer program will save us some time in cataloging, and here is one example where indeed it does do just what we hoped it would!

Before we move on, let's look one more time at a catalog record first in the public display format and then in the MARC record format. Figures 4.7 and 4.8 are records

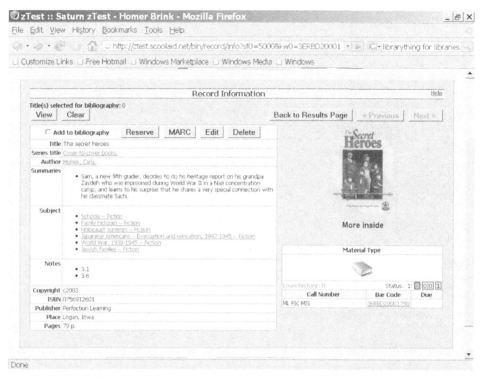

Figure 4.7.   Public display for the book *The Secret Heroes*. Reprinted with permission from OPALS.

for the book *The Secret Heroes* by Carla Mshek and Margo Sorenson. Figures 4.9 and 4.10 are for the audio book *Sunday Mornings in Plains* by Jimmy Carter. Take some time to compare both the public display and catalog records for each item and then look at the records as they compare to each other including different subfields in similar fields.

After a quick look at this record, we notice right away that there are no punctuation marks; no colons, semi-colons, or slashes. Some programs automatically insert all of that stuff for us so we don't have to remember a space, colon, space after the title proper. This is good for us, but remember that not all programs do this.

You see a couple of fields in this record that we have not discussed. It is not because those fields are not important; it is just that they have less to do with retrieving the record for our users than some of the other tags we've discussed and so I skipped them in discussing the MARC record. Considering the fields we have discussed, notice the 082 tag for the Dewey Decimal Classification number that tells us that the 22nd edition of the unabridged DDC was used to create this number. You would have to check your abridged edition to decide if you wanted to keep this number or not. We see the 245 field has two people in the subfield c for the statement of responsibility. We notice that there is no semi-colon between the two names, and so we know that both people had the same job; but we only see one name (Carla Mshek) in the 100 field. To find our second author, we have to find the tracings for other statements of

Figure 4.8. Catalog record for the book *The Secret Heroes*. Reprinted with permission from OPALS.

responsibility. In the MARC record, that information is located in the 700 field. If we look down the record, we see Margo Sorenson in the 700 tag with a date after her name in the subfield d. Sometimes, in creating an authority record for a person, we need to know their birth and/or death dates. If you don't know this information don't look for it. However, if you have that information on the item, you will probably want to include it as it is included here in our example. Go back up to the 245 field and notice the second indicator "4" and notice too that the title begins with the initial article "the" and so we have to tell the computer to skip those four spaces and file this record under the letter "s" for "secret."

As to the other fields, we see some 500 fields that have not been discussed before. In the notes area, there are specific 500 (or, as we say generically, the 5XX) tags that are assigned for specific information. In our example we see the 521 field, which is used to describe the audience for this item. In our example, our book has been written with a third-grade vocabulary (the first 521 note) and will be of interest to readers in the third to sixth grades. We know this because of the first indicators in the 521 tags. Unfortunately, our public display is not much help for our user. Now you know if you see something cryptic like this that the note is referring to grade level of vocabulary and interest. Parents and teachers often want to know what grade level the book has

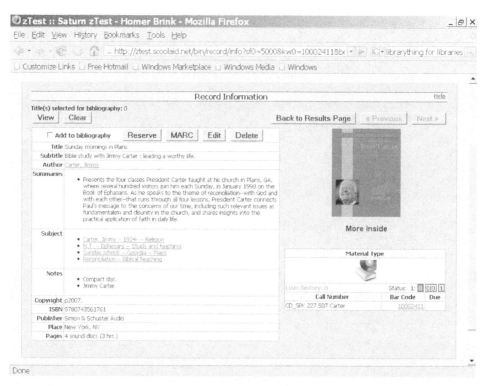

Figure 4.9. Public display for the audiobook *Sunday Mornings in Plains*. Reprinted with permission from OPALS.

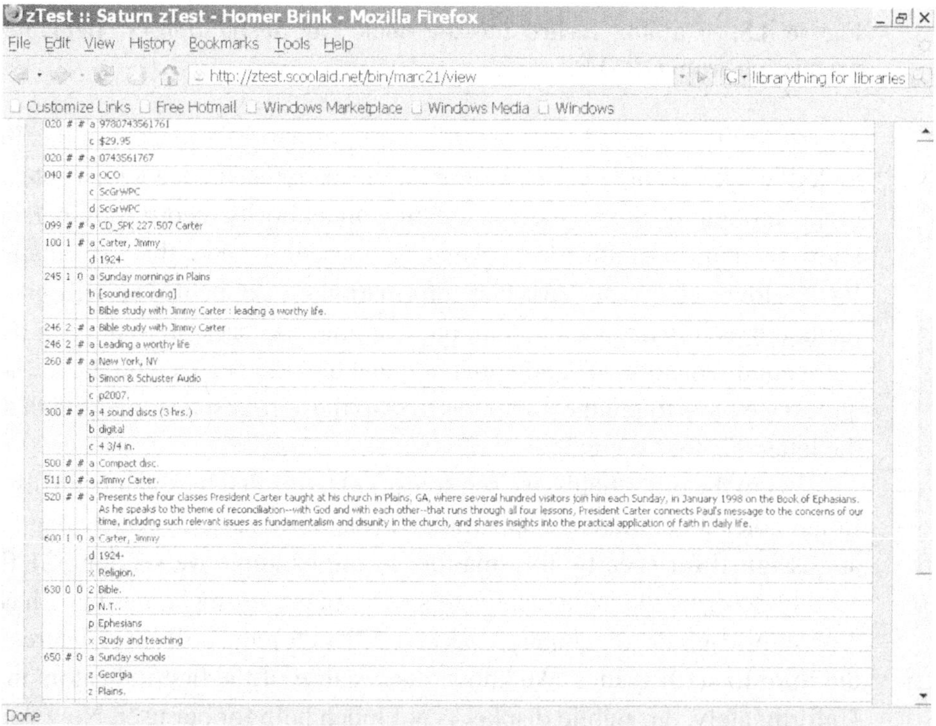

Figure 4.10. Catalog record for the audiobook *Sunday Mornings in Plains*. Reprinted with permission from OPALS.

been written for. Understanding the 521 field can help you answer this question for them. If you are cataloging and you want to make note of something, it is all right, not desirable but all right, to simply use 500 for each one of the notes. However, you should know that there are specific tags for specific notes as shown in this list:

- 500: title and format information; other general information as needed;
- 504: if item includes a bibliography and index (but index alone goes in a 500 note);
- 505: for contents notes;
- 508: notes about how the item was put together: directors, producers, program designers, etc.;
- 511: performer notes;
- 520: summary notes;
- 521: audience as in movie ratings or other audience level information;
- 538: system notes; what the computer program needs to run;
- 546: language; if item has sound track in one language and captions in another, if item as been translated from one language to another, or if item is in a non-English language;
- 586: awards note; example, Academy award, book awards such as Newbery or Caldecott, etc.;
- 590: local notes such as an autographed item or problems with the item such as missing pages

Again, when in doubt, using the 500 field is acceptable cataloging.

The 650 fields are our topical subject headings. We know that there are different kinds of subject headings as we discussed in chapter 2. We have to tell the computer what kind of headings we are using. So, as in the case of the 5XX tags, we have different 6XX tags for different types of subject headings. The most commonly seen subject heading fields are 650 (topics), 651 (places), and 600 (people as subjects). In this example we have only 650 fields, or subject headings about topics such as "Holocaust survivors" and "Japanese Americans." All of these subject headings end with a subfield "v," which is used to tell the genre of the item. A genre subdivision, such as "fiction," is used to help our user know what kind of item is being described. Besides the call number in the 082 field that tells us this is in the fiction section of our collection, the subject headings can also be used to note what kind of item is being displayed. In recent years, catalogers have also used a 655 field to describe the genre of the item, but even now, that field is not seen very often in MARC records.

Let us now look at Figures 4.9 and 4.10 and see what the public and catalog records look like for a non-book item and see what is the same and what is different between these records and our book item records.

By now we should be fairly comfortable with these records. Both the public display and catalog records are very similar to those of our book records. No 082 field exists, but we do have a local call number in the 099 field. In the MARC format, a tag that includes the number "9" means that it is presenting information made up by the cataloger that may not follow standard rules. In this case, the 099 tag tells us that the library has made up a local call number that is different from the standard number in the 082 tag. Most systems will allow you the option to use the 09X local classification field without having to delete the 082 field. We notice that this item has a funny classification. Part of it is familiar (227.507), but there is stuff in front of that number (CD_SPK) that we do not recognize. Librarians often have their non-book materials in separate places in the library and note this separation by adding prefixes to the classification number. In this case, we can guess that "CD_SPK" means that this item is a CD and it is a spoken recording (audiobook) rather than a movie or music. That's our guess, and remember, our guess is as good as our users' guesses. Keep this in mind when creating non-standard cataloging for your items. If you are confused by something like "CD_SPK," then your users may also be confused.

Our 245 tag includes the subfield h to define the type of non-book item this is. No problem there; we're used to that already. However, what are those two 246 fields? Remember our tracings for other title information? Look up at Figure 4.9 and see in the public display where it says "subtitle." The 246 field allows us to trace for other title information. So if someone wants to look for the audiobook by Jimmy Carter and does a title search for "bible study with jimmy carter," that user will find the right item because we have traced for that subtitle.

We have two 6XX fields that we may not recognize. First we see the 600 field with Jimmy Carter's name. You may ask, well if Jimmy Carter is listed as the author in the 100 tag, why do we also see his name as a subject heading? We see his name in the 100 field because he is responsible for the intellectual content of the item but also we see his name in the 600 field because this item is *about* him as well. Be careful not to confuse the 100 and 600 fields. Remember, the 100 field is because the person wrote the content of the item and the 600 field is because the item is about that person. Finally, we see a 630 field. Without getting too technical, the 630 field says, this item is about a book and here is the title of that book. This is a typical field to see in an item about the Bible, but otherwise we don't see it very often in most catalog records.

CONCLUSION

In this very technical chapter, we've made a brief excursion into the land of MARC. We know that it is a format for getting information from the item to the computer database, but it is not the standard for cataloging. We know it is a little intimidating at first, but once we've seen a few examples, we should be at least a little bit comfortable with where the information goes for title, publisher, physical description, some notes, and subject headings.

In chapter 6 we will look at places we can go to get library programs that will help us keep our library materials organized. We will also find out how to get free catalog records and how to finish off the process of cataloging an item.

Points to Remember about Chapter 4

- MARC is the computer language to get the information from the item to the computer database.
- The rules that apply for cataloging according to *AACR* apply to MARC records.
- The common fields for a MARC record are:
  - 082—Dewey Number
  - 020—ISBN
  - 100—Author
  - 245—Title and statement of responsibility
  - 246—Tracing for other title information
  - 250—Edition
  - 260—Publication information
  - 300—Physical Description
  - 440—Series title
  - 5XX—Any number of notes; using 500 only is acceptable although not preferable
  - 6XX—Any number of subject headings (600, 650, 651 most common)
  - 700—Tracing for other persons responsible for the content of the item
- Indicators, the numbers between the field number and the subfields; if nothing else, watch for the second indicator in the 245 field to make sure it is instructing the computer on what to do if the title begins with "the," "a," or "an."
- A good resource to go to for more information about the MARC format is the Library of Congress guide at: http://www.loc.gov/marc/umb/

PROBLEM SET

1. Take this information and put it into a MARC record format:

   Title and statement of responsibility: *John Adams* written by David McCullough. Published by Simon & Schuster in New York in 2001. It has 751 pages, illustrations, and stands 25 centimeters. It is about President John Adams (see if you can find at least two subject headings). It will be classified under Biographies using the abbreviation "BIO." The ISBN is 0684813637. It includes a bibliography and an index.

2. Take this information and put it into a MARC record format:

   Title and statement of responsibility: *The Broker* by John Grisham.

   This is a work of fiction. It was published by Random House Audio in New York in 2005. It contains five CD-ROM discs that run about six hours and was recorded digitally, and the discs are the standard 4 3/4 inches. The narrator is Dennis Boutsikaris. On the item it says it is abridged from the original print edition.

Here is the summary statement that you can copy into the correct field: John Grisham delivers another legal thriller of unparalled suspense. With fourteen years left on a twenty-year sentence, notorious Washington power broker, Joel Blackman, receives a surprise pardon from a lame-duck president. He is smuggled out of the country on a military cargo plane, given a new identity, and tucked away in a small town in Italy. But Blackman has serious enemies from his past. As the CIA watches him closely, the question is not whether he will be killed, but rather who will kill him first.

In terms of subject headings, you'll want a genre heading for fiction, but you'll also want to add the genre subdivision (subfield v) to the subject headings you decide on. The item is about an American in Italy and it is a suspenseful story.

ANSWERS

1. This is an actual book, and the MARC record from the Library of Congress in a slightly abridged format follows the explanation below:

    Don't forget that you can use the Library of Congress web site (http://authorities.loc.gov/ or http://catalog.loc.gov/) to find your subject headings. Notice we have the standard 082 tag but we have provided our own call number in a 092 (modified DDC number) tag. This problem doesn't have any tricks to it except perhaps in the 082 classification field with the cutter of "B" for biography rather than cuttering for "McCullough" or even for "Adams." In working with biographies, it is often the case that you will see that if a biography is classified under the discipline rather than in a biography section; then the cutter will be "B" for biography rather than for the author or subject of the biography. I have a personal preference for cuttering first for the subject of the story, in this case for Adams, and, if need be, a second cutter for the author of the work, in this case McCullough. If I was cataloging this book, I might be tempted to classify it either under BIO for biography or the classification number 973.4 for American history and then add ADA MCC. In this way, all of my biographies of John Adams are together. But again, this brings out the art, rather than the science, of cataloging.

020 __ **a** 0684813637

082 00 **a** 973.4/4/092

    a B

    2 21

092 ## aBIO ADA (we might opt to write Adams' name full out)

100 1_ **a** McCullough, David G.

245 10 **a** John Adams /

    c David McCullough.

260 __ **a** New York :

    b Simon & Schuster,

    c c2001.

300 __ **a** 751 p. :

    b ill. ;

    c 25 cm.

504 __ **a** Includes bibliographical references and index.

520 __ **a** The story of the life and times of the second president of the United States, John Adams.

600 10 **a** Adams, John,

    d 1735-1826.

650 _0 **a** Presidents

    z United States

    v Biography.

651 _0 **a** United States

    x Politics and government

    y 1775-1783.

651 _0 **a** United States

    x Politics and government

    y 1783-1809.

2.   Again we have an example of a real audiobook and again it is adapted for our purposes:

020 __ **a** 0739316443

092 __ **a** FIC GRI

100 1_ **a** Grisham, John.

245 14 **a** The broker

      h [sound recording] /

      c John Grisham.

260 __ **a** New York :

      b Random House Audio,

      c p2005.

300 __ **a** 5 sound discs (ca. 6 hrs.) :

      b digital ;

      c 4 ¾ in.

511 0_ **a** Read by Dennis Boutsikaris.

500 __ **a** Abridged.

500 __ **a** Compact disc.

520 __ **a** John Grisham, delivers another legal thriller of unparalled suspense. With fourteen years left on a twenty-year sentence, notorious Washington power broker, Joel Blackman, receives a surprise pardon from a lame-duck president. He is smuggled out of the country on a military cargo plane, given a new identity, and tucked away in a small town in Italy. But Blackman has serious enemies from his past. As the CIA watches him closely, the question is not whether he will be killed, but rather who will kill him first.

650 _0 **a** Americans

    z Italy

    v Fiction.

650 _0 **a** Attempted murder

    v Fiction.

650 _0 **a** Ex-convicts

    v Fiction.

650 _0 **a** Pardon

    v Fiction.

651 _0 **a** Italy

    v Fiction.

655 _7 **a** Suspense fiction.

    2 gsafd

655 _7 **a** Legal stories.

    2 gsafd

655 _0 **a** Audiobooks.

700 1_ **a** Boutsikaris, Dennis.

The first thing we notice is the exceptionally long summary statement. Someone really went to great lengths to give us a good summary of the story. We're glad for that because it helps us to create our subject headings. Other than that, there are no real surprises in this record.

CHAPTER 5

What You Need to Know about Local Cataloging Problems

We've been talking about how to create original bibliographic records using MARC and *AACR*. **Original cataloging** means that you are putting all of the information about your item in a blank record without using any other records from any other library or database. Most of the time you will be cataloging materials that other librarians have already cataloged and you can do what we call copy cataloging (see next chapter). However, many, perhaps most, small libraries also have very special collections; copies of local cookbooks, local histories, school yearbooks, and the like, that have been self-published and that probably do not exist in any other library collection. These can be tricky items to work with, and so we have here a chapter devoted to your own special collections. In cataloging your own materials, you have to do your own leg work; checking for the authority of the name of your author, the subject headings, and even the classification number.

Self-published books can be problematic for a number of reasons; they may not have title pages or publication data such as publisher names and dates, or they may not even have page numbers. Local history books and cookbooks can also be a problem because they may not be easily classified. Lots of smaller libraries simply keep local publications on a shelf in the back room because they are so difficult to catalog.

However, we now know that access to information is very important to our users, and so, with this in mind, we will explore some shortcuts in dealing with these types of items in terms of classification, subject headings, and physical description, to get them out of the back room and onto the shelves.

Before discussing the different aspects of cataloging local materials, we have to discuss the differences between local interest items and local authors. It may be that someone in our neighborhood has written a story of fiction that takes place far away from our community. It may also be that that same person has written a non-fiction history about our community. When cataloging these items we have to make a policy. We have to decide if all local materials will be in one place; that includes items about the community as well as items written by community members even if the items themselves are not about the community. We could make two separate sections: a local author section and a local interest section. However, what about our example above? Do we have one local collection that includes both local interest as well as local authors? Do we have two separate collections? Or do we simply arrange the items according to standard cataloging rules and hope that our subject headings help our users find what they are looking for? One thing to consider is the general availability of the items. If you have rare books, such as school yearbooks and other non-commercially produced materials, then you may well want to have a special collection so you can keep closer look out for those items.

In the art of cataloging, even something that looks pretty clear to us is open for discussion and reconsideration. Take a look at your local collection and ask yourself how you think your users might access these items. It may well be that you decide you don't want a "local collection" but rather you want your locally produced items interfiled with all of the other items. However, you may also decide that when your users come into your library looking for local publications (about the community or by community authors), they want those items shelved together in one place. The choice is yours, but you will need to make a choice that you can be comfortable with and stick with for the foreseeable future. The rest of the chapter will include references to MARC formatting; remember that you can go to the MARC21 web site (http://www.loc.gov/marc/bibliographic/ecbdhome.html) to follow along with the information being presented here.

CLASSIFICATION

Remember that in classifying an item, we are supposed to think about the discipline covered by that item. So a book on the genealogy of a local family would probably be classified under 929, for genealogies, or maybe 929.4, for personal name genealogy. A book that is a compilation of letters home from a soldier in World War I is likely to be classified under 940.4 for the time period of history covering the years of World War I. Finally, a book on a description of a particular geographical area that

900 History, geography, and auxiliary disciplines
910 Geography & travel
920 Biography, genealogy, insignia
930 History of ancient world to ca. 499
940 History of Europe   Western Europe
950 History of Asia   Orient   Far East
960 History of Africa
970 History of North America
980 History of South America
990 History of other part of world, of extraterrestrial worlds   Pacific Ocean islands

Figure 5.1.   Summary table for 900 classification.
Reprinted with permission; © OCLC, 2004.

includes a description of the land as well as recollections of the history of the area by local residents would probably be best classified under 917 for geography of the United States. The common link in the books we described above is the 900 number. Recall from Figure 1.3 in chapter 1 that 900 is the classification number for History and Geography. Let's take a closer look at that number here in Figure 5.1. Notice that the numbers range from general geography to specific geographical locations, including "extraterrestrial," or outer space.

Our Dewey classification table tells us that the 900s are used for "the story of events that have transpired, or an account of the conditions that have prevailed, in a particular place or region."[1] Basically this means that if the events being described are of a place or thing that happened in the past, then the 900 classification is the number you want to use. So let's take a look again at our examples of the local genealogy, letters from a World War I soldier, and the description of a place.

At first, we thought all three of the items described at the beginning of this chapter should be classified in three different places, and indeed, this is correct. However, what if we want all of our books of local interest to be together in one place? We won't muddy the waters right now by including items by local authors that are not about our local community; we are just talking about locally produced items that are about our local area.

It is perfectly reasonable for our users to want all of the local information to be in one place and reasonable for us to use one classification number for that purpose, even if it may not be exactly "correct" according to classification standards. In thinking about the use of discipline for deciding on a number, we can argue that our users are interested in local history and geography; therefore the discipline is the number for the place in which we are living. For those of us reading this book in the United States, that puts us in the number range of 974–979. The 974–979 numbers are used for regions of the United States as well as for individual states, with the exception of Hawaii, which is part of the Pacific Islands and therefore has the number 996.9. Figure 5.2 provides a summary of the numbers for the regions and states of the United States. Keep in mind that this is only a summary; to be sure you have exactly the right number, you should consult a DDC book.

973   History of America

(We are not including some subdivisions of this number here because the purpose of this chart is to show the numbers for local regions, not the numbers for American history.)

974   Northeastern United States

974.1   Maine

974.2   New Hampshire

974.3   Vermont

974.4   Massachusetts

974.5   Rhode Island

974.6   Connecticut

974.7   New York

974.8   Pennsylvania

974.9   New Jersey

975   Southeastern United States

975.1   Delaware

975.2   Maryland

975.3   District of Columbia

975.4   West Virginia

975.5   Virginia

975.6   North Carolina

975.7   South Carolina

975.8   Georgia

975.9   Florida

Figure 5.2.   900 classification for the United States.
Reprinted with permission; © OCLC, 2004.   (*Continued*)

976   South central United States

      976.1   Alabama

      976.2   Mississippi

      976.3   Louisiana

      976.4   Texas

      976.6   Oklahoma

      976.7   Arkansas

      976.8   Tennessee

      976.9   Kentucky

977   North central United States

      977.1   Ohio

      977.2   Indiana

      977.3   Illinois

      977.4   Michigan

      977.5   Wisconsin

      977.6   Minnesota

      977.7   Iowa

      977.8   Missouri

978   Western United States

      978.1   Kansas

      978.2   Nebraska

      978.3   South Dakota

      978.4   North Dakota

      978.6   Montana

      978.7   Wyoming

      978.8   Colorado

      978.9   New Mexico

Figure 5.2.   (*Continued*)

979   Great Basin and Pacific Slope of United States

    979.1   Arizona

    979.2   Utah

    979.3   Nevada

    979.4   California

    979.5   Oregon

    979.6   Idaho

    979.7   Washington

    979.8   Alaska

Figure 5.2.   (*Continued*)

The information in Figure 5.2 is taken from the *Abridged Dewey Decimal Classification*. The unabridged version of DDC provides for more specific geographic information. For example, using the information from Figure 5.2, if we want to classify an item about the region of upstate New York, all we can use is 974.7. However, using the unabridged version of DDC, we can get a more detailed number; specifically 974.773, which helps us pinpoint the focus of the item just a bit more. For a smaller library collection, if you have already decided to use the abridged edition of DDC, you need to stick with it and be satisfied with cataloging only down to the state level rather than down to regions of a state. Additionally, if you have an item that covers more than one state, you need to use the number for the larger region. For example, if you have a book on the geography of the Pacific coastal region of the United States, which includes Oregon and Washington, you need to use the number 979.

Let's take another look at those letters from our World War I soldier. Notice that the number we suggested, 940.9, is not part of that 974–979 number range. Letters are considered "personal narratives" and so are kept with the number for the particular historical time period. War letters are classified under the number for the war. The number for letters from World War I is 940.9; the number for World War II is 940.5309. These two wars affected the entire world but started in Western Europe and so are classified under Western European history. In contrast, letters from soldiers involved in mostly U.S. conflicts are classified under the periods of United States history. So letters from a Civil War soldier would be classified under 973.7; letters from a soldier fighting in Vietnam would be classified under 973.923; and letters from a soldier in Iraq would be classified under 973.931. We've supplied here the more common war numbers, but to find numbers for other conflicts, take a look at the Library of Congress database. Remember, the Library of Congress uses the *unabridged* Dewey Classification numbers, so you will probably find yourself cutting the number somewhere around three or four numbers after the decimal. Again, having the abridged DDC in front of you is really valuable especially when dealing with local materials where you will find the need to create your own numbers more critical than when dealing with most commercially produced items.

It appears then that with the exception of personal narratives about the two World Wars, we can easily use just the local geographical classification for our local items, right? Well, maybe not. What do you do with cookbooks that have been published by local community organizations? They certainly should not be classified under the history number. While we might argue for geographic classification, to use the regional 900 number really is upsetting us because it just isn't right. We know that cookbooks, unless they are about local foods of the region, really have nothing to do with the location and should actually be classified under the number 641.5. Even a cookbook about regional foods still belongs in the 600 classification as DDC allows us to use the cookbook number (641.5) and add the regional number. For example, a cookbook about food from Delaware would be classified under the number 641.59751. Notice that the geographic number (975.1, which we got from our Figure 5.2) is added to the main number (641.5), but the second decimal point is dropped because we can only have one decimal point. So instead of having 641.5975.1, we drop the second decimal point to get the number 641.59751. We can only add a geographical number if the DDC book instructs us that this is all right to do. Under cookbooks, we are told we can add the geographic location for cooking about specific places.

Classifying our cookbooks under the number for cooking is more correct than using a local 900 number, but it messes us up because now we can't justify putting the local cookbooks with other local interest items. Or can we? Sometimes librarians will use prefix abbreviations to pull items together that do not have the same classification number but belong together on the shelf. We see this most often with reference materials. In this case we see "REF" in front of the classification number. This is perfectly legal to do, and we might consider doing that before we consider giving our entire local items the same classification number. In this case, you probably want to use a prefix for the classification number so that your users, and other library workers, know that these are items of local interest and shelved in a different place, not with the rest of the regular collection. For example you could use the prefix "LC" for "Local Collection" in front of the classification numbers like this: LC 641.59751. One caveat to make here is that the prefixes are often missed by library users and shelvers. If you do use the prefix and you are having a hard time locating an item that is not checked out, go to your "regular" shelves and look there. Chances are very good the item was not shelved correctly and is sitting with the non-local interest items.

You need to decide on a cataloging policy for your library. Either you catalog all of your local items under one classification number, which is reasonable but not exactly correct cataloging, or you use the rules of classification and classify your local items under the discipline covered in the items. Many librarians use prefixes with their classification numbers, so this is not an odd cataloging practice and you should feel comfortable in making this choice.

What you should not do is assume that your local collection of 20 books will always be a collection of just 20 books and so you do not need to classify them at all. A common mistake of new catalogers is to think of the collection as a static collection of materials that will always stay the same number. But collections grow; especially local collections of special items that will probably never be weeded out of the collection. So if you look at your collection now and say to yourself, "Well, I only have 20 local histories so I might as well just use one number," you are making a mistake. You need to consider the future, especially as it becomes easier for people to publish their own materials. If you have a small collection now, chances are pretty good that the collection will grow in the not-too-distant future. So take a look at your collection, decide how it can be most easily classified, how it can be most accessible to your users, and how much it will grow in the future, and then make a decision you can stick with in terms of assigning classification numbers.

SUBJECT HEADINGS

Whether you opt for a simple classification scheme (meaning all local items go in the classification number for the state) or you decide to classify your items according to the discipline, the subject headings for these items are vitally important. You should make it a general practice to use a subject heading for your area for all of your local items that defines the geographic location of the content of the item; that is, a geographic heading for your city or state. When you do this, you are providing for your users, through the library catalog, a way to know what the local items are in the library regardless of the discipline or content area of the item. What this means is that all of your local items, whether they are war letters, cookbooks, local histories, or any other local interest items, will all have the same geographic subject heading along with the other necessary subject headings for the individual items. In a sense you are putting your items all on the same subject area "shelf." Let's look at some examples and see how this works.

Let's say your local items are about Tivoli, New York. You need to see if this is a location that the Library of Congress has established so you can use that heading. If we look at the LC authority database under "tivoli n.y." we see that the established heading according to *LCSH* is "Tivoli (N.Y.)" and so we can add a geographical subject heading (651 field) using that heading.[2] But what if our city has not been established by the Library of Congress? The Library of Congress doesn't like for us to make up our own topical subject headings but is a little more tolerant when it comes to geographic subject headings.

The Library of Congress publishes a multi-volume manual that gives us instructions for using and even constructing "legal" subject headings, including a form to send in to suggest new subject headings.[3] Volume one includes directions for creating geographic subject headings. The directions are long and involved and difficult to condense here. Suffice to say, if we need to create a heading for a city that has not been established by the Library of Congress, then we have the power to do so using the name of the city and the abbreviation of the state. *Sears* also allows for the construction of new geographic place names and gives us a model to follow to do so.[4] Here's an example of creating our own geographic subject heading. Let's say our city is Belmont, Wisconsin. If we search the LC database, nothing comes up under that name. Instead of panicking, we follow the *Sears* model of "Chicago (Ill.)" and come up with "Belmont (Wis.)" as our geographic subject heading. In your public library in Belmont, Wisconsin, you now know that you can add a geographic subject heading (651 field) to all of your local interest items, and when your users come in looking to see what you have about the community, a simple subject search will bring all of those materials together! The great thing about cataloging standards is that this will work for all places that do not have LC authority records, from Cactus (Tx.) to Phair (Me.). Most importantly, you need to have a geographic heading for your local materials regardless of their content.

In a recent tour of public libraries, I found out that many public libraries collect the neighborhood school yearbooks; mostly the high school yearbooks. The books are collected but kept in the back room, uncataloged, and the librarians sigh that they are taking up space and no one ever looks at them. We could create a simple bibliographic record with the title of the yearbook and the name of the school in the statement of responsibility and even as the publisher, but what do we do about subject headings?

Let's look at an example of a high school yearbook from Theodore Roosevelt High School in Los Angeles, California. You want a subject heading that is specific for that city as well as the school. *Sears* doesn't have a listing for Los Angeles, California, but, as we noted above, in the introduction for using *Sears* headings, we are instructed to use "Chicago (Ill.)" as a model for creating subject headings for other cities. Looking at Chicago (Ill.) and thinking about the discussion at the beginning of this section we know that we can also use "Los Angeles (Calif.)" for the name of our city for this yearbook. We check this at the Library of Congress under their subject authority database (http://authorities.loc.gov/webvoy.htm) and we see "Los Angeles (Calif.)" as an authorized geographic heading. As for the name of the school, if we do another search on the LC subject authority database for "theodore roosevelt high school" we are happy to see that LC has already created a subject heading for this school: Theodore Roosevelt High School (Los Angeles, Calif.). We are really happy about this! But we should remember that for our local collection, if we don't find a heading for the local schools or other organizations in our community, finding headings like this one will help us to create our own because we can use them as models for the headings we need to make up.

We now have a geographic subject heading and we have a name subject heading for our school, but what subject heading do we use to tell our users we actually have school yearbooks? If we go back to the LC subject authority database we find we have two choices. First, we can use the subject heading "School yearbooks"; and second, we can use the name of the school with the subdivisions "Students—Yearbooks," which would look like this: Theodore Roosevelt High School (Los Angeles, Calif.)—Students—Yearbooks. It's one of those unfortunate subject headings that tell us exactly what it is that we have but no one in a million years would think to look for. Would you look for yearbooks under the name of the school, students, and THEN yearbooks? Depending on our collection, we may decide to simply use the name of the school. If, however, we are collecting both the yearbooks and the school newspapers, we might decide to use the fuller subject heading for the yearbook and use the heading for the school with the subdivision "Periodicals" for the newspapers just to help our users to be more precise in their search.

One advantage *Sears* has over *LCSH* is that it recognizes that our users might want to look for things first as place and second as subject. In *LCSH*, the topical subject heading for school yearbooks can have a geographic subdivision added to it, which would look like this: "School yearbooks—Los Angeles (Calif.)." *Sears* recognizes the importance of local subject headings and allows us to use the local geographic heading first with a subdivision for the topic, like so: "Los Angeles (Calif.)—School yearbooks."[5] Below are examples of what these headings would look like in the MARC format catalog record.

Our example is the student yearbook from Theodore Roosevelt High School, in Los Angeles, CA. Here are suggested subject headings in MARC and how the information looks in the **online public access catalog (OPAC)** for this title:

MARC:

610 20 $a Theodore Roosevelt High School (Los Angeles, Calif.)

$x Students

$v Yearbooks.

OPAC:

Theodore Roosevelt High School (Los Angeles, Calif.) – Students – Yearbooks.

- Recall from our discussion in chapter 4 that there are several different types of subject heading fields. In chapter 4 we discussed the 600, 650, and 651 fields as the most common of the subject fields. This field, the 610, is for what librarians call "corporate names." Corporate names can be names of corporations like IBM or Apple Computers, but corporate names can also be names of things like schools, office buildings (like the Empire State Building), and ships (like the Titanic). The subfield "x" we see is for a topical subdivision, and the subfield "v" is for genre or form of the item, in this case it is a yearbook. The subfield "v" is fairly new in its use, so if you are looking at older MARC records, you might see a second subfield "x," which is perfectly all right.
- Notice the indicators in this field: The first one, "2," tells us that this is a heading with the name of the corporation in what we call "direct order," which is similar to the way we would speak naturally. The second indicator, "0," tells us that this is a Library of Congress subject heading. To make sure you are using the right indicators, you can go the MARC web site for this field: http://www.loc.gov/marc/bibliographic/bd6xx.html.

- Remember that the subfields are code for the computer to understand what you are trying to tell it. The OPAC line shows us what our users would see.

MARC:

650 _0 $a School yearbooks

> **$z Los Angeles (Calif.)**

OPAC:

School yearbooks – Los Angeles (Calif.)

- This is a typical topical subject heading. The geographic subdivision (subfield "z") is in this subject heading because of the directions the Library of Congress provided that states that you may add a geographic subject heading to this topical heading. The problem is that you would only know that if you had the print version of *LCSH* in front of you. This is one of the biggest problems of using only the online *LCSH* for your subject headings. If you looked up "school yearbooks" in the authority database you would never know that you could add a geographic subdivision. If you did a basic search of the LC catalog (http://catalog.loc.gov/) you might get the idea that "school yearbooks" can have a geographic subdivision on it. But, then again, you might not.
- The indicators show us that this is again a Library of Congress subject heading (by the "0" in the second indicator place). The first indicator is blank, meaning no information is being supplied about the subject heading. We have several choices for the first indicator, but we are best off by simply leaving it blank.
- Notice that this subject heading does not end with a period (.). That is because it has a parenthesis at the end of the line, which serves as our final punctuation.

MARC:

651 _0 $a Los Angeles (Calif.)

651 _7 $a Los Angeles (Calif.)

> **$x School yearbooks.**

> **$2 sears**

OPAC:

Los Angeles (Calif.)

Los Angeles (Calif.) – School yearbooks.

- Yes, we have two geographic subject headings here. All of the 6XX fields may be repeated.

- Our first geographic subject heading is for the name of the city (Los Angeles). Recall that we thought it would be a good idea to add a geographic subject heading for all of our local interest items.
- For our first example, the first indicator is blank and the second indicator (0) tells us that this is a Library of Congress geographic subject heading. However, the second indicator in our second geographic subject heading is different. This one has a "7" for the second indicator as well as a subfield, "2." This is because we are using the *Sears* subject headings for this field and we need to tell other catalogers. Our users will not see the subfield 2 and really don't care if we are using *LCSH* or *Sears* or making things up, but other catalogers care, and that's why we bother with the indicators. If you use a second indicator, "7," you have to have a subfield "2" to define the list you are using.
- Notice that in this second geographic subject heading, the heading ends with a period (.) after "yearbooks." This is because the subfield, "2," is not part of the subject heading. As the OPAC line shows, our users will see: Los Angeles (Calif.)—School yearbooks. They will not see the subfield "2."
- The second geographic subject heading is helpful if you have yearbooks from different school in Los Angeles (or whatever area you are in) because it pulls together all of your yearbooks from Los Angeles regardless of which school published the yearbook. By using this geographic subject heading, your users see all the different school yearbooks you own.

We need to also look at subject headings for our local cookbooks. The Library of Congress uses the unfortunate topical subject heading "Cookery" for cookbooks. Try this: Go up to one of your library users and ask, "If you were looking for a cookbook, what subject heading would you use?" Chances are really low that your user will say, "Cookery." One day we can hope that, for the Library of Congress, "cookery" will become "cooking," but until that time, you will want to use the *Sears* subject heading "Cooking." Make it a practice when you get new cookbooks in your collection and when updating cataloging for older materials to add the *Sears* topical subject heading "Cooking." It will look like this in your MARC record: "650 _7 $a Cooking. $2 sears" just as we saw in our examples above. *Sears* allows us to add a geographic subject heading to "Cooking." If, for example, we had a cookbook of foods from Newark, Delaware, that was published by the Visitor's Bureau for the city of Newark, Delaware, we could use the subject heading "Cooking—Newark (Del.)" which would look like this in a MARC format: 650 _7 $a Cooking $z Newark (Del.) $2 sears (if the book contains regional recipes of the entire state, then you would just use "Delaware").

As we mentioned above, *Sears* is kind to us and allows us to essentially "collect" our local items together by place first and topic second. You can approach all of your local materials in this way. Note that this is for local collections only and that you should not make a habit of turning over or reversing the order of all of your subject headings. However, for your local items, you could in fact have something in your catalog that looks like this:

- Newark (Del.)—Cooking.
- Newark (Del.)—Folklore.
- Newark (Del.)—Genealogy.
- Newark (Del.)—World War, 1939–1945.

Your users will appreciate the fact that they can easily identify all of the local materials in the OPAC. If you pull your materials together using the subject headings, you have more freedom to use more precise classification numbers because you will not feel the need to shelve everything together even if you have a local collection prefix to your classification number. This is an example of how to use subject headings to pull together items that have a similarity but would not normally show up together on the shelf.

PHYSICAL DESCRIPTION

This brings us to describing the item itself. If you go to the local bookstore and pull a book off the shelf, chances are very good that book is going to have a cover and a title page. Now go back to your library and look at your locally produced books. Chances are really good that those books do not have a title page. Furthermore, we'll be really lucky to see any kind of information about where, when, or who published the book in our hands. This is the sad fact about local publications and a big reason why many of us decide to not catalog them at all. The following is not a foolproof approach to cataloging locally produced publications, but it should help you to approach the problem so you are not nervous about cataloging them.

Chief Source of Information

Remember that we learned that in cataloging books, the front and back of the title page are pretty much the only places we can go to when describing the item. What if you don't have a title page? Here is where the use of brackets and notes will come in handy. Figure 5.3 shows a book cover for a collection of letters written by a soldier in World War I and locally published. No title page, no statement of publication, and no page numbers exist. Because this provides us with a lot of problems, we're going to use this as our example. *AACR* tells us that when there is no title page we can take the information from the book cover or any other part of the item that gives us a clue to the information we are seeking as long as we make a note of the source of our information.[6]

Title and Statement of Responsibility

Looking at this cover, we see a very long title, and we are a little unsure of how to approach it. Unfortunately this is a kind of tricky title, and equally unfortunately,

MERVILLE E. HARRINGTON
(January 6, 1901 - February 28, 1919)

PRIVATE FIRST CLASS

COMPANY H

FOURTH INFANTRY

NEW YORK GUARD

LETTERS HOME
(September 4, 1918 - February 20, 1919)

Figure 5.3.   Local publication: Letters Home.

it is common to see such convoluted titles on self-published books. Our librarian has opted for "Letters Home" as the title. One might argue that "Merville E. Harrington" is the title because that appears at the top of the cover of the book. Either choice is understandable. "Letters Home" makes a logical choice because it is more descriptive of the content of the book than is "Merville E. Harrington" and because "Letters Home" appears in larger and darker type than the other information on the cover. If we went with the title "Merville E. Harrington," then our users might think this is a biography

Title choice one:

Letters home (September 4, 1918 – February 20, 1919) : Merville E. Harrington

(January 6, 1901 – February 28, 1919) private first class Company H Fourth Infantry

New York Guard / [compiled by Byron Merville Harrington]

Title choice two:

Merville E. Harrington (January 6, 1901 – February 28, 1919) private first class

Company H Fourth Infantry New York Guard : letters home (September 4, 1918 –

February 20, 1919) / [compiled by Bryon Merville Harrington]

Figure 5.4.   Title and statement of responsibility choices.

of Merville when really it is a collection of his letters. In recognition of the art of cataloging, I will give you examples of either choice here in Figure 5.4 and you can make your decision according to your own comfort level.

First, notice the use of capitalization. Remember that proper nouns, such as the name of a military unit, are capitalized.[7] As directed by *AACR,* we leave in the parentheses as they appear on the cover of the book.[8] Now, notice in both of our examples the statement of responsibility: "[compiled by Byron Merville Harrington]." Your first question is why isn't Merville the author and your second question is why is "compiled by Bryon Merville Harrington" in brackets.

To answer your first question, Merville is the author but doesn't end up in the statement of responsibility because his name is already in the title.[9] As to your second question: We know that Byron put the letters together because right after the cover of the book is a note from Byron telling us who Merville was and why Byron put the letters together in this book. We use brackets around the statement of responsibility because there is no title page that tells us Byron is the compiler; we've taken this information from a source other than the chief source of information.[10] Using brackets tells other librarians (if not also our users) that we made up the information; it is not actually part of the item at all.

For either choice, we need to make added title and author tracings. Figure 5.5 shows us how our choices would look in a MARC record format with tracings for authors and other titles. Remember that in making your own MARC record, you can only have one author (100) field and one title (245) field, so don't let the two examples confuse you.

Both of our records have tracings for both Harringtons; Merville in the 100 field for main author and Byron in the 700 field for additional author. Both records have 246 fields that contain information from the subfield "b" in the 245 field as well as some modified information from the subfield "a" of the 245 field. All 246 fields have the same indicators. The "1" in the first indicator place tells the computer to make a note

Title choice one:

100 1_ $a Harrington, Merville E.

245 10 $a Letters home (September 4, 1918 – February 20, 1919)

: $b Merville E. Harrington (January 6, 1901 – February 28, 1919) private

first class Company H Fourth Infantry New York Guard

/ $c [compiled by Byron Merville Harrington]

246 10 $a Letters home

246 10 $a Merville E. Harrington (January 6, 1901 – February 28, 1919) private

first class Company H Fourth Infantry New York Guard

246 10 $a Merville E. Harrington private first class Company H Fourth Infantry

New York Guard

500 __ $a Cover title.

700 1_ $a Harrington, Byron Merville.

Title choice two:

100 1_ $a Harrington, Merville E.

245 10 $a Merville E. Harrington (January 6, 1901 – February 28, 1919) private

first class Company H Fourth Infantry New York Guard

: $b letters home (September 4, 1918 – February 20, 1919)

/ $c [compiled by Bryon Merville Harrington]

246 10 $a Letters home (September 4, 1918 – February 20, 1919)

246 10 $a Letters home

500 __ $a Title taken from cover.

700 1_ $a Harrington, Byron Merville.

Figure 5.5.   MARC format for title choices for Letters Home.

about this title and an added entry. The computer is supposed to pull this up if a user is doing a title search even though this isn't the 245 field because of the "1" in that first indicator place.

The second indicator value of "0" means the information in the 264 field is part of the title information found in the 245 field. Who cares about this information? Well, another cataloger might, but your users probably don't; nevertheless, you need to include the right values in this and all fields. Notice some of the 246 field information is just the difference between including or not including information from the cover that is enclosed in parentheses. Look especially at the 246 field that reads: "246 10 $a

Merville E. Harrington private first class Company H Fourth Infantry New York Guard." Here we have taken great liberties in taking out Merville's birth and death dates.

The 246 field helps us to provide alternatives of title searches for our users. *AACR* tells us we can omit long title information if the information being omitted is not included in the first five words of the title and if it does not omit essential title information.[11] It is possible that someone might do a title search without including Harrington's dates, and so we're allowing for that possible search by creating an additional 246 field. Finally, notice the two 500 notes in the two different examples. Both notes are correct, although the first one, "Cover title.," is more correct. Technically speaking, "cover title" is the cataloger's way of saying "title taken from cover." So you see both are correct; the first one (the one your users may not understand) is the library way of saying that the title did not come from a title page.

Publication Information

The next part of the record is the publication information. We have a statement at the beginning of this book that is essentially a letter from Byron about why he put this collection together. He signed the letter with his address. That is all we know about the place of publication for this book. Additionally, when the book was received by the library, someone stamped a date on it. This isn't much to go on, but take a look at possible 260 fields for this book:

- 260 __ $a [Norwich, NY? :$b s.n., $c 2007?]
- 260 __ $a [Norwich, NY? :$b Byron Merville Harrington?, $c 2007?]

Having all of the information in brackets with the question marks tells other librarians that we are really guessing about all of this information. In fact, take a look at the $b information; "s.n." in our first example. This means that there is no name of a publisher (s.n. is Latin for "sine nomine," meaning there is no name on the item), and we're not even attempting to say who published this. In our second example we are guessing (and probably rightly so) that Byron was the publisher. We use the date "2007," assuming that the item was new when it got that received date stamp. If you have an item in your collection that looks really old but has a new date stamped in it, you would guess that it wasn't new when it was given to the library. If that's the case, you need to try as hard as you can to guess at least a century in which case you can use something like "19??" or "18??" but do try to make a guess. If you really have no idea, you can use "n.d." for "no date." If you know of some information but not others, you can mix the use of the brackets and question marks like this:

- 260 __ $a [Norwich, NY] :$b[Byron Merville Harrington?],$c2007.

This shows that we know it was published in Norwich, NY, but the place of publication did not come from the title page. We are not sure that Harrington did the publication, but it's our best guess. The only thing we are sure of and that came from our chief source of information (pretending we actually have a title page) is that it was published in 2007. The point is that when we are guessing or supplying information we want everyone to know we are guessing.

Page Numbers and Illustrations

The pages in this book are not numbered. When children's books have pages that are not numbered, we get to say "1 v." for the pages. But if an adult book has unnumbered pages, we have to count them. If we count the pages then we record that information in brackets. This book has a portrait of Merville and some other illustrations. Older cataloging will have specific type of illustration information like "port., ill." For newer cataloging, all you need to do is note that there are illustrations using the abbreviation "ill." This book measures 29 centimeters. With all of this information then, here is what our 300 field will look like:

- 300 __ $a [96 p.] :$b ill. ;$c 29 cm.

This shows that we counted 96 pages (counting front and back) in this book, and we include this in brackets because they are not numbered. The rest of the information should look familiar to you: There are illustrations and the book measures 29 centimeters.

Notes

As hinted at in our discussion of title and statement of responsibility, we need to account for our decisions in cataloging this book, and we do this in the 500 notes area of the record. We must have a note that says we are using the cover for the title. We might want to add a note about the lack of a title page and how we know about the publisher, but the only required note is that for the title:

- Required note:
  - 500 __ $a Cover title.
- Optional additional note:
  - 500 __ $a This book has no title page and only a letter (p. [3]) stating why the letters were published signed by the compiler with no publication information given.

Of course we will want some kind of summary (520) field; something to help our users realize what they have brought up in the OPAC and to help with key word searching. In his statement about why he put these letters together, Byron includes a paragraph that makes this sound like a very exciting book to read. It is all right to take a direct quote from some place on the item as long as you include it in quotations marks as you would for any quotation. Our first example includes a summary statement taken entirely from the book itself:

- 520 __ $a "Merville's letters reflect his precarious age. A boy far from home for the first time, trying to be a man. He struggles to deal with homesickness, cold, parasites, and disease. He makes friends and he meets some unsavory characters" (p. [3]).

While this is quite a teasing and appealing summary statement, it doesn't help much with key word searching. Here is a more traditional type of summary statement for a non-fiction work, but remember, as a cataloger you can design your own summary notes:

- 520 __ $a Collection of letters from Merville Harrington to his family when he was a soldier during World War I as part of the New York Guard and stationed at Stone Ridge, High Falls, and Peekskill, New York.

Clearly this second example is more academic than and not nearly as exciting as the first example, but look at all of the key words that will help in retrieving this item: Harrington, World War, and New York. It isn't pretty, but it will surely be more useful to your users.

This completes our look at the bibliographic record for a locally produced item. Figure 5.6 shows us what a MARC record might look like for this item assuming we use "letters home" as our title.

All of these fields have already been discussed, but some information bears repeating here. For the classification number we used the 900 table; we get the classification for New York State *OR* we can use the number for the conflict (940.4), which would be the more correct number unless it really confuses our users (both numbers are presented here but in a real bibliographic record you would have to select one); the Cutter (subfield "b") came from the OCLC Cutter site (see chapter 1); subfield "2" notes the edition of the abridged DDC (noted in the first indicator) used to create the number.

When we used Merville Harrington as a subject heading (600 field), notice that the second indicator is a "4," which means this is not a Library of Congress authority name. We looked up Harrington in the LC authority database but he wasn't there, so we constructed his name as best as we could and used the second indicator to tell other catalogers that we made this one up. Notice we did not include the dates for Harrington. Normally one only includes dates if they are needed to identify one person from another; since Merville seems to be all alone, there is no need to include his dates either here or in the 100 field.

Some final thoughts about subject headings: Notice that there are a lot of subject headings in this record, and that's all right. How did we get all of those headings? If you don't have a copy of the five volumes of *LCSH,* you can go to the LC database and look to see if other books like the one you have, have been cataloged and see what subject headings were used. Remember that the second indicator in the 6XX fields tells us the list that was used to create the heading. We know that most of these subject headings are LC-created and approved headings. However, the last two geographic

082 14 $a 974.7   **OR** $a 940.4

    $b H299 2007

    $2 14

100 1_ $a Harrington, Merville E.

245 10 $a Letters home (September 4, 1918 – February 20, 1919)

    : $b Merville E. Harrington (January 6, 1901 – February 28, 1919) private first

    class Company H Fourth Infantry New York Guard

    / $c [compiled by Byron Merville Harrington]

246 10 $a Letters home

246 10 $a Merville E. Harrington (January 6, 1901 – February 28, 1919) private first

    class Company H Fourth Infantry New York Guard

246 10 $a Merville E. Harrington private first class Company H Fourth Infantry New

    York Guard

260 __ $a [Norwich, NY?

    :$b Byron Merville Harrington?

    ,$c 2007?]

300 __ $a [96 p.]

    :$b ill.

    ;$c 29 cm.

500 __ $a Cover title.

520 __ $a Collection of letters from Merville Harrington to his family when he was a soldier during World War I as part of the New York Guard and stationed at Stone Ridge, High Falls, and Peekskill, New York.

600 04 $a Harrington, Merville E.

650 _0 $a World War, 1914-1918

    $v Personal narratives, American.

Figure 5.6.   Letters Home MARC record.

(Continued)

650 _0 $a World War, 1914-1918

$z New York (State)

$z Chenango County.

650 _0 $a World War, 1914-1918

$z New York (State)

$z Greene.

650 _0 $a Soldiers

$z New York (State)

$z Greene

$v Correspondence.

650 _0 $a Soldiers' writings, American.

651 _0 $a Greene (N.Y.)

$v Biography.

651 _0 $a Chenango County (N.Y.)

$v Biography.

651 _7 $a Green (N.Y.)

$x Soldiers.

$2 sears

651 _7 $a Chenango County (N.Y.)

$x Soldiers.

$2 sears

700 1_ $a Harrington, Byron Merville.

Figure 5.6.   (*Continued*)

subject headings have second indicators with "7" as the value. This means that some other list has been used, and if we look a little further, at the subfield "2," we see that the list that was used was the *Sears* list. Remember that *Sears* understands local collections and lets us pull together all of our items about the town of Greene in the county of Chenango in the state of New York with topical subdivisions. The Library of Congress does not allow this, but *Sears* does, which is one more reason why it is nice to have a copy of the *Sears* book in your library.

NON-BOOK ITEMS

Books are not the only locally published items. In this day and age of the Internet, there are lots of local residents who are putting together web pages of local interest. Sound and video recordings of local citizens are housed in our libraries. Sometimes even local art work is donated for circulation in our libraries. We've discussed cataloging various non-book items in chapters 3 and 4. You can take a similar approach to these items as you do to book items; try to find a creator (author), a logical title, and a way to describe the physical aspects of the item. Subject headings will be pretty much the same as they are for book.

CONCLUSION

The information in this chapter is meant to help you with original cataloging problems you will probably run into when dealing with locally produced items. We discussed school yearbooks, local histories, and cookbooks. Other types of local publications will cause you to wrinkle your brow and frown with confusion. The points you should remember are: creator/author; title; production/publisher; classification; and subject access. Keep those points in mind and you should be able to attack your local publications.

Points to Remember about Chapter 5

- Locally produced items almost never have all of the information we wish they would have, like a title page, publication information, etc.; therefore they are harder to catalog and will almost always require original cataloging.
- It is worth the time to catalog locally produced materials to provide access to them for our users.
- Classification: Decide if all local materials will:
  - Be classified by discipline and not be shelved together;
  - Be classified by discipline with a prefix to keep them shelved together;
  - Be classified by geographic numbers and shelved together.
- Subject headings: add geographic subject headings to locally produced materials as needed, including city/town and county if need be.
- For items that do not have the right chief source of information, you must make notes about the source of your title and other information as needed.

NOTES

1. For a description of what should be included under the 900 History classification see the *Abridged Dewey Decimal Classification,* 14th ed., 2004, p. 102.

2.   Remember, in searching for place names, to use the state abbreviations as described in chapter 2, Figure 2.5.

3.   The instructions for using the Library of Congress subject headings are provided in the two-volume set *Subject Headings Manual* published by the Library of Congress. A new edition is set to be published by the end of 2008. For more information, see the LC web site at: http://www.loc.gov/cds/lcsh.html.

4.   For instructions on model or "key" subject headings, see *Sears List of Subject Headings,* 19th ed., 2007, p. xli.

5.   See page xxv in the introduction to *Sears.*

6.   This section depends heavily on the standards established in *AACR.* In order to keep the flow of the text from being interrupted by constant references to the *AACR* rules, we will make use of this notes section. If you have access to a copy of *AACR,* feel free to follow along in that book. See *AACR* for directions on using information besides the title page (or other chief source of information), found in chapter 1 "General Rules for Description" under rules 1.0A2 and 1.1A2.

7.   Again we turn to *AACR* to check our rules for capitalization; here we go to the appendix for guidance, specifically, rules A.13E3 and A.18B1.

8.   *AACR* tells us to record the title as it appears on the title page (or other place depending on what we have) and so we would include the parentheses, any misspellings, etc.; whatever we see, that's what we record according to rule 1.1B1.

9.   *AACR* has several rules about a statement of responsibility being included in the title proper; for more help see rules 1.1B2, 1.1E4, and 1.1F3.

10.   Fortunately, *AACR* understands that not every item is published according to cataloger's rules and therefore gives us the opportunity to look beyond the chief source of information as long as we make proper notes about it; see rules 1.0A2, 1.0C1, and 1.1F1.

11.   It's not very often we have to deal with really long titles in new works, but as already discussed, one never knows what your locally produced title is going to look like, so we're glad to have *AACR* rule 1.1E3 and 1.1E4 to help us deal with this problem.

CHAPTER 6

What You Need to Know to Organize Your Collection

At this point you should have a pretty good feel for how to describe an item both in terms of what it is (physical description) and in terms of what it is about (intellectual description). Of course none of this information is any good without some way of providing access to the collection as a whole.

If we go back to our grocery store, we might see a large sign hanging from the ceiling that tells us where we can find specific types of products. It might tell us, for example, that bread is in aisle five and cat food is in aisle six. This is a very simple form of collection access. In a library, we want our users to be able to find very specific items, and so we need a library system to help us out. In the old days, this system would have been the card catalog filled with 3" × 5" cards that contained the bibliographic record for each item. Today, we make use of computers to help us provide access to our collections.

When libraries first went through the automation process, many started with individual parts of the system, beginning with automating the cataloging process. Next to be automated were the circulation and collection access processes. Today, most library programs will automate the entire process all together. A system that automates the cataloging, acquisition, circulation, and public access parts of the process is call an **integrated library system**, or **ILS**. This means that the computer program has a component that allows one to catalog the collection, circulate the items, and provide access through an online public access catalog (OPAC).

In this chapter we will explore some of the types of library systems that are available to us. We will present information about some of the available products, but it must be stressed here that the products noted are examples only of the types of systems available; this is not an exhaustive list and there is no endorsement of any of these products implied here. We are only providing a starting place for you to think about ways of providing your users with access to the collection. The resource list in Appendix B includes a few books and articles you can read to find out more about library systems. Asking around your area or on library discussion lists is also a good way of finding out success and failure stories for specific systems.

Whether you decide to go with an open source or commercial program, you have to remember that records do not show up automatically. You have to find some way of getting the information about your collection into your computer program. If you don't already have your collection automated, but you do have catalog cards for your items, you will want to seek out a company (like Brodart or MARCIVE) to convert your paper records to an electronic database. If you don't have any cataloging at all, you will enter original records or copy records from other databases into your new automated system. This is an expensive process either through buying the conversion from a company or spending your time (or the time of another staff member) to enter all of the data. Make sure you have the time and money to do this correctly and accurately to save you problems later on.

OPEN SOURCE PROGRAMS

Not very long ago, if you wanted an automated library system, you had to spend a lot of money. About 20 years ago, open source software started appearing on the Internet. The premise of these programs was that people should be able to see how a program worked instead of blindly accepting a program and not being able to change it for one's own purpose; sort of like giving the professional access to go under the hood of a car and make changes to the engine as needed. The GNU Project (see the web site: http://www.gnu.org/) initiated this idea, and from there more and more programs developed to address this problem. In recent years, programs such as OPALS, LibLime, and LibraryThing for Libraries have created a situation wherein one could actually catalog, and in some cases circulate and provide access to a collection, without spending any or at least very little money. Keep an eye out for these open source programs as they will become more and more popular, especially as budgets get tighter and tighter.

One outcome of the Internet, electronic data, and open source systems is something called "social cataloging," which usually takes into consideration the standard cataloging rules but also allows for something called "tagging." Tagging is where the "social" part comes into play. People who contribute to these social catalogs may or may not be catalogers or even librarians; often they are just folks who have some item or interest in an item. Their contribution to the tagging is in the introduction of terms to connect to the item that may or may not be rooted in any standard cataloging scheme. Take for example our topical subject heading "World War, 1914–1918." We look at this and sigh, knowing that we have to teach our users that if they are interested in World War I, they have to use the dates to find it. Tagging allows for a great deal of flexibility, so an item about World War I can have, for example, these terms connected to it:

20th century   air warfare   **aviation**   great war   **history**   military
military aviation   **military history**   war   warfare   **wwi**

These tags are from the Danbury (CT) Library site linked from LibraryThing for Libraries. I looked up the book, *The First Air War, 1914–1918,* by Lee B. Kennett. The result was a traditional record as we've discussed in previous chapters with the added tags we see above. The popularity of the terms is shown by the size of print; for example, "aviation" appears in the database more often than does "Great War." This is mentioned here because open source programs tend to allow users to add tags and you might see these if you look as some of the open source programs.

A few open source programs are described here. The inclusion or exclusion of a program is in no way an endorsement of one program over another. Experts in this field are arguing the pros and cons of open source programs. Besides cost, the biggest advantage of the open source programs is that of flexibility. These programs are designed to meet individual needs, and so one can either change the program if it resides on your own computer system or request changes that will be met in a timely manner. I am simply presenting some examples of programs available to you. A Google or Yahoo search under "open source library systems" will yield a lot of further reading for you should you need to know more about this.

- LibraryThing (www.librarything.com/): LibraryThing went "live," that is, became active on the Internet, in 2005 and is what we call a "social cataloging" application. It was created by Tim Spalding, not a librarian, with the idea in mind that people might want to organize their personal home collections and could benefit from seeing the things other people collect. Some libraries have joined LibraryThing for Libraries (www.librarything.com/forlibraries/) where, for a fee, their collections are made available to the general public via the Internet. The fee charged is dependent on the size of the collection; "small libraries" may store their collection of up to 5,000 for $15 per year. Sounds great, but this is not an integrated library system; you still need some way to circulate your items.
- OPALS (www.opals-na.org/): OPALS began in early 2000 in New York State and within just a few years has become a popular response on library lists as an answer to the question, "Is there an affordable ILS out there?" OPALS, developed from the library world, shows all of the qualities librarians look for in

traditional commercial programs; it is an integrated library system, it provides collection and circulation reports typically needed by librarians, and it has the look of a traditional OPAC. The fee for the subscription to the service is usually less than $1,000 per year.

- LibLime (liblime.com): LibLime also came from the library world but is spearheaded by CEO Joshua Ferraro, who has his roots in open source programming. It too began in early 2000 with "Koha," which is also described in a very positive light on library discussion lists. The company offers services for all library types from the very small public to the large academic. Again, the fee for technical support services varies according to the size of the collection.

Open source programs are most certainly the wave of the future in library automation. To make the most use of this type of software, one should have good knowledge of cataloging trends and standards. However, even without this knowledge, an open source program can be easy to use and much more reasonably priced than commercial programs.

COMMERCIAL PROGRAMS

If your library is part of a library consortium or group, chances are pretty good that you will be told which program to buy for providing access to your collection, or one will be supplied for you. If you are not part of a larger library system and you have money to purchase a commercial system, you should give it some consideration. Most commercial programs have been around for decades and so have gone through the test of time. There is no assumption that you want to "get under the hood" of the program or have much knowledge of library systems at all.

Again, the programs described here are simply a sample of the programs available, and no endorsement is implied:

- LibraryWorld (www.libraryworld.com): LibraryWorld is not your typical commercial program, but it isn't open source either. It is a very inexpensive ILS that has all of the components you need to organize and circulate your collection. It has the benefit of a free 30-day trial where you can test the system and see if you like it; that is a big bonus. However, be cautious about the catalog program. It does not have any prompts as to how to enter your data, so if you don't know about your indicators and subfields, you are in trouble. However, at $365 per year, the price is right.
- Book Systems (booksys.com): Book Systems provides a suite of modules for library automation needs including Atrium, Concourse, and eZcat that together form your integrated library system. Providing services since the 1980s, Book Systems offers the flexibility to choose the products you need for your library.

- Right On Programs (rightonlibrarysoftware.com/index.html): Right On Programs have been around since 1980; they are a suite of separate modules so that a small library can decide to use only the cataloging or only the circulation systems if it wants to. Right On also has a card-printing program if you do not want to automate your card catalog (create an OPAC). The programs run from $600 to a little more than $1,000 depending on the program and whether the access is a single computer or a network.

COPY CATALOGING

Both open source and commercial programs come equipped to take in different types of cataloging. Original cataloging is what you do when you create the bibliographic record yourself. So far, that is the type of cataloging we have been discussing. However, there are lots of bibliographic records out on the Internet, and many of them can be downloaded to the computer system you are using. When you copy a record from one library or database to your own, you are doing what librarians call **copy cataloging**. The advantage of copy cataloging is that you don't have to create the record yourself. Copy cataloging cuts down on the time spent cataloging your collection and frees you up to spend more time with your library users. But beware: Not all records are created equal.

One reason you need some knowledge about cataloging is so that you can be a wise consumer of other cataloging. For example, now that you know the benefits of a 520 field, you can look at a record and say to yourself, "Well, this is a good record, but it's missing a summary statement (520 field), so I'll download the record and then add a summary statement myself." You also need to be able to determine the difference between good and not-so-good bibliographic records; those that are worth downloading and updating and those that are better skipped. At this point you should be able to recognize when a record has the minimal amount of information to be useful: the author, title, physical description, and subject headings. So you should be able to tell if you are looking at a good record or not.

When you go looking for catalog records to download, you need to think about who is doing the cataloging. If you go to the Library of Congress for cataloging, you can be pretty sure that the records are of high quality. Likewise, if you have access to World Cat (http://www.worldcat.org) from OCLC you will have access to literally millions of bibliographic records. However, like other databases that have contributors from more than one library, you might run into duplicate records. Although you have access to all of those records, unless you have access to World Cat from a local academic library you cannot get to the MARC records, so it is not the best place to go to for copy cataloging. For cataloging children's materials records, especially non-book items, a good database is the state database from Florida called SUNLINK (http://www.sunlink.ucf.edu/). But select those records carefully, as there is a variety of quality of cataloging on that site. For example, go to that site and search for "Harry Potter and the Order of the Phoenix." How many records do you get? How many for the book? The sound recording? The movie? In this case, you will need to look at more than one record and make a decision about which one is the better record. The web site LibDex (http://www.libdex.com/) provides a list of library databases that are searchable online. Unfortunately it only sorts them by country and not by library type, and there are a lot of libraries in the United States!

Other online databases such as LibraryThing modify the cataloging standards or do not use them at all. If you use these records, examine them very carefully. Review each bit of information and be especially careful about accepting subject headings. Some databases do not use the standard subject headings at all. If there is a MARC record, take a good look at the tagging information for *LCSH* or *Sears* information just to make sure you have a standardized subject heading.

PROCESSING ITEMS

Once your items are in a computer database and accessible through an OPAC you need to get them on the shelf. If you are using an ILS, then you need to put a barcode label on your item somewhere for circulating the item and for inventory purposes. The barcode is entered as part of the bibliographic record. Most library programs just have a line that reads "barcode" or "item number" as the place holder for the barcode. The barcode is what connects the catalog record to the circulation database. The type of program you have will dictate the type of barcode you use. The first purpose of the barcode is to automate the circulation process. The user takes the item to the circulation desk, and by using a barcode reader or typing in the number, you check the item out electronically. The second purpose of the barcode is to keep accurate count of your collection. Your ILS program should include a way of entering the barcode to conduct an inventory of your collection; that is, to keep track of your items and see which ones have gone missing during the course of the year.

The barcode may be added in a number of places. For book items, some librarians put the barcode on the inside front cover so that it is easy to get to but hard to pull off. Some librarians put the barcode on the back upper-right corner or front upper-left corner of the book so it is easy to get to for inventory purposes. Placement of the barcode on non-book items may be a little trickier.

For DVDs or other items in cases, you can follow the same practice you use for books. Items in a package, such as children's reading bags including a book, toy, and tape cassette or CD, can be really troublesome. Packages of materials can be tricky because you may be tempted to barcode each item in the package for purposes of easy inventory. However, keep in mind that in check-out if you barcode each part of the package then you must also enter the barcode of each item to check out each part of the package. This makes for a time-consuming practice. You are probably best off simply applying a single barcode to the entire package. You might end up with sticking the barcode on an index card, laminating the card, and attaching the card to the bag. If you do this, you should also make a label for the package that lists each item found in the package and then in check-out and check-in, make it a practice to make sure the package is complete.

You want to try to develop a standard practice so you always know where the barcodes are located on any item type so that when checking things out or conducting an inventory, you don't have to go looking for it.

With or without the ILS, you will need a spine label with the call number of the item on it so that you know where to shelve the item. Traditionally, the spine label goes on the book spine approximately one-half to one inch from the bottom of the book. Again, non-book materials may pose a problem regarding where to place the label. The label should be easy to read from the shelf, so keep that in mind when deciding where to put the label. Sometimes you have no choice but to put the label in a place that will not show up once the item is on the shelf. This is an unfortunate reality of cataloging; simply do the best you can to strive for most spine labels to be easily read from the shelf. For both the barcode and the spine label, make a decision about where the labels will be placed and stick to it. Nothing is more frustrating than having to flip through a book to find a barcode or searching the item to find its call number.

CONCLUSION

This then concludes our brief exploration into the realm of cataloging. We have discussed the physical and intellectual ways of describing an item. We have discussed how to deal with problems specific to our own collections. We have discussed ways of getting copy cataloging for the items we have so we can spend more time with our users and how to process the materials once they have been cataloged. As explained in the introduction to this book, we are not giving you all the information you will ever need to become an expert cataloger, but we hope you now have enough information to be an informed consumer of cataloging and to be able to deal with the special items in your collection.

Good luck and happy cataloging!

Points to Remember about Chapter 6

- Open source programs are probably the wave of the library automation future; they are web-based and tend to be on the less expensive side, charging mostly for server space and technology support.
- Commercial programs have a longer history than open source, but the expense of the programs will always be a major factor in deciding between commercial and open source programs.

- Regardless of the type of program you select, you are better off with an integrated library system than with separate modules that may or may not "talk" to each other.
- Copy cataloging is a good way of getting records for your items if you don't order them with cataloging, but beware of bad "copy" and always check records before downloading them to your database.
- When processing your items, be as uniform as possible in the placement of the call number labels and bar code labels.

APPENDIX A

Glossary of Technical Terms

AACR: Most common way of referring to the standards for cataloging used in the United States and in many countries throughout the world. These are the rules followed when creating the catalog record. Currently the rules are in the second edition, revised, and may be referred to as *AACR2*, *AACR2r*, or *AACR2 revised.*

Anglo-American Cataloging Rules: See *AACR*.

Authority File: The list or database of terms that are accepted by the cataloging agency, which could include personal names, names of corporations, subject headings, or even titles.

Bibliographic Record: See *Catalog Record*.

Call Number: The entire number on an item that shows the classification (see) as well as the Cutter for the item.

Catalog Record: The place where information about each item is written down either on a physical 3" × 5" card or in the online database.

Chief source of information: The part of the item from which information for the physical description is taken; for books this part is the title page and the back of the title page.

Classification: A way of arranging information; in libraries, classifications are often shown on items in terms of numbers, letters, or a combination of numbers in letters that show, in shorthand, how the items are arranged.

Controlled Vocabulary: A list of words and phrases agreed upon by a group of experts as the words used to describe the subject of an item. *Library of Congress Subject Headings* (see) and *Sears List of Subject Headings* (see) are the two major lists used in public and school libraries.

Copy Cataloging: Creating a bibliographic record using a record from another library or database, usually consisting of only updating or adding specific information about the item; see also original cataloging.

Cross Reference(s): In authority records, the directions to go from one term to another, directing from an invalid term to the valid term or from a broader term to a more specific term.

DDC: See *Dewey Decimal Classification.*

Dewey Decimal Classification (DDC): The system used to organize items on the shelves by using numbers to represent the names of disciplines; for example, 636.8 for an item about cats as pets.

Field: Each line in the MARC record noted by a number containing information about the item being cataloged; also known as a Tag.

ILS: See *Integrated Library System*.

Indicators: The numbers or blanks between the field number and the subfield information that tells the computer what to do with the upcoming information.

Integrated Library System (ILS): Computer program that allows for multiple library functions usually including cataloging, circulation, and the *Online Public Access Catalog* (see).

Intellectual Content or Description: In cataloging this refers to what the item is about rather than describing the format of the item; the parts of the catalog record that describes the intellectual content of the item are the areas of subject headings and classification.

Key Words: Any word used to describe an item without recognition of controlled vocabulary lists; words found in the catalog record or otherwise used for information retrieval in online programs.

LCSH: See *Library of Congress Subject Headings*.

Library of Congress Subject Headings (LCSH): The list of controlled vocabulary developed by librarians at the Library of Congress; the list is recognized as the authority for assigning subject headings to describe the intellectual content of the item.

MAchine Readable Cataloging: See *MARC*.

Manual: The part of DDC that helps to define the use of specific numbers; especially helpful when trying to decide between numbers for related topics.

MARC: Stands for MAchine Readable Cataloging and is the system created by the Library of Congress when cataloging items electronically; the language used to take information from the item being cataloged through the cataloging rules (*AACR*) and into a computer database so our users can find information about what we have in our libraries online. MARC is *not* a cataloging system but rather is the program used to create catalog records following standardized cataloging rules.

Online Public Access Catalog: See *OPAC*.

OPAC: The computer or web-based program that allows library users to search the library's collection electronically.

Original Cataloging: Creating a new bibliographic record without any other cataloging copy (see also copy cataloging).

Physical Description: A description of an item based on what it is rather than what it is about; what the item looks like. For example, the number of pages, the length of a movie, or the size of the poster.

Public Display: The way the catalog record looks to the user, without the markings of the MARC computer code.

RDA: The name of the proposed new cataloging standards due out sometime after 2009. The new standards will focus on the intellectual content of the item rather than on the format of the item. The argument is that "Harry Potter and the Sorcerer's Stone" should have one catalog record regardless of whether one is talking about the book, movie, or audio-book.

Resource Description and Access: See *RDA*.

Schedules: The listing of the Dewey Decimal Classification numbers from 000 to 999.

Sears List of Subject Headings: Like *LCSH*, this is a controlled vocabulary of subject headings but it was designed for use by catalogers in school and public libraries.

Standard Subdivisions: The most frequently used of the tables, the standard subdivisions (also known as Table 1) can be applied to almost any number without specific directions from the schedules. Standard subdivisions include format of the item (dictionary, magazine, index) or the focus of the item (the topic from a historical point of view or as it affects a given population).

Subfields: The separate lines in the fields of the MARC format, noted usually by a letter but also can be numbers.

Subheadings: When used with subject headings, these are words or phrases that show more detail about the subject matter of the work.

Summaries: The major classes of the Dewey Decimal Classification system shown from the Ten Main Classes to the Hundred Divisions to the Thousand Sections; this section of DDC immediately precedes the *Schedules* (see).

Table 1: See *Standard Subdivisions*

Tables: In DDC, the tables are used to further define format and focus (Table 1), geographic or people emphasis (Table 2), literary type (Table 3), or linguistic emphasis (Table 4) of a work. The table numbers are never used alone and are almost always assigned only if directed to do so from the schedules.

Tag: See *Field*.

Tracing: The term given to ways of "tracing" or finding information about an item, including subject headings, series titles, additional authors, performers, etc.

Work Mark: Usually the first letter of the first word of the title added to the cutter number to differentiate two publications by the same author in the same year so that the call number is unique for each publication.

APPENDIX B

Annotated List of Helpful Resources

Appendix B includes a list of helpful resources to keep you cataloging. However, there is no substitute for talking with others to solve cataloging problems. Check out your state library association; most state associations have sections for different types of libraries. Discussion lists such as those for paraprofessionals offered through the American Library Association (see http://www.ala.org/ala/mgrps/rts/lssirt/index.cfm); or PUBLIB, a discussion list for public librarians (see http://lists.webjunction.org/mailman/listinfo/publib) can provide help, at least a friendly ear to listen to the problem, and suggest resources for help. The following are other resources that may prove helpful to you.

DEWEY DECIMAL CLASSIFICATION SYSTEM

Many sites (mostly school sites for school children) help in understanding the organization of DDC. OCLC, which owns the copyright for DDC, offers a number of resources and links for helping to understand DDC including:

1. The glossary of DDC terms: http://www.oclc.org/dewey/versions/abridged edition14/glossary.pdf
2. The introduction to the full edition of DDC: http://www.oclc.org/dewey/ versions/abridgededition14/intro.pdf
3. Introductions to DDC for K12 kids as well as for adults: http://www.oclc. org/DEWEY/resources/public.htm; and
4. A short biography of Mr. Dewey himself: http://www.oclc.org/dewey/ resources/biography/default.htm.

CATALOG RECORDS

These sites help one to understand how to use MARC for cataloging materials. There is not much "friendly" information online for understanding the cataloging rules themselves.

1. A good introduction to the design of bibliographic records is provided by the Library of Congress under the title "Understanding MARC Bibliographic" and can be found at this site: http://www.loc.gov/marc/umb/.
2. To follow the changes that are expected to come from the new cataloging rules (RDA) see this site: http://www.collectionscanada.ca/jsc/.
3. To create a catalog database for a small cost, see Open-source Automated Library System (OPALS) at this site: http://www.opals-na.org/. This is not the only open source program, and we predict to see many more in the future, but it is easy to use even for the person with very little professional training. Chapter 6 provides the names of other programs that are available as well.
4. One book that has been written to simplify the cataloging rules is *The Concise AACR 2,4th edition,* by Michael Gorman based on *AACR2 2002 Revision, 2004 Update* published by the American Library Association in 2004. Even though there have been many updates to *AACR*, including a full 1998 revision, this small book can be helpful in trying to understand the workings of *AACR*. Although the book is written to explain the rules, one must remember that it is written for librarians and so there is a lot of library vocabulary included in the text of the book.
5. The Library of Congress maintains a site with all of the MARC tags and codes. It is written by librarians and for librarians, but it can be a helpful source of information if you really get bitten by the cataloging bug. That site is located at: http://www.loc.gov/marc/bibliographic/ecbdhome.html

OPEN SOURCE CATALOGING PROGRAMS

1. Marshall Breeding provides an unbiased and excellent (although fairly technical) web site to keep up with library automation trends that also serves as a good place to see which programs are being used in public libraries. See the web site: http://www.librarytechnology.org/.
2. "Open Source Library Systems: Getting Started" by Dan Chudnov is a good (although a bit technical) article about open source programs and can be found at http://www.oss4lib.org/readings/oss4lib-getting-started.php. Even though the article is 10 years old, it has a good description of the history of open source library systems.
3. "Open Source" Integrated Library System Software by Richard W. Boss was posted on the Public Library Association Tech Notes page on June 24, 2008, and can be accessed at: http://www.pla.org/ala/mgrps/divs/pla/plapublica tions/platechnotes/opensource2008.pdf.

APPENDIX C

MARC Record with Corresponding *AACR* Rules

The MARC record is divided roughly into 14 areas. Presented here are the more common fields with an explanation of the *AACR* rules that relate to those fields. After the annotated record, a plain MARC record without explanation will follow in Appendix D. For a complete list and explanation of each MARC tag, see the Library of Congress web site for MARC21 Format; Bibliographic Data at: http://www.loc.gov/marc/biblio graphic/ecbdhome.html. Each field discussed is described in terms of its number (for example, 245 field) that is followed by spaces for the indicators, and then the subfield area. Each subfield (usually a letter such as a, b, or c) is preceded by a mark to tell the computer that new subfield information is about to be presented. The form of this mark will depend on the system. We are using the dollar sign ($) here, but it could also be the number sign (#), a double bar sign (|), or some other character. We are also listing each subfield on a new line. Again, the way you see this information is dependent on your system. The system you are using may run one subfield into the other.

LEADER AND VARIABLE CONTROL FIELDS

The "front" of the MARC record begins with what are called "fixed fields" that contain mostly computer code for the type of item being cataloged. There are no corresponding *AACR* rules to the fixed fields because it is all computer code rather than description of the item. The fixed fields are presented here because they are part of the record, but with one exception (the 06 space in the leader) this area can be left alone. This part of the record also includes numeric data, the future of which is uncertain. It has been hoped for a long time that the information in this area would be searchable, but systems just haven't caught up with the hopes of the librarians. We will not go into detail on these fields but present them to you so you recognize them when you see them. Note that the fields here do not have indicators or subfields.

Leader or 000 Field

This information includes information about the creation of the catalog record and the type of material being cataloged. Each part of this field is counted as a space beginning with 00 and ending with 23. Not every space is defined, which means some are left blank. In our example here we will bold the space that is important to us and use the underscore (_) to note the undefined, or blank, spaces. In most systems, this field will be noted by the title "Leader" or by the field number "000." Remember that this field is not part of the physical description and therefore has no corresponding *AACR* rule to help understand the meaning of the tag.

> **Leader: 01361cam_a2200301_a_450_** We are interested in the 06 space (remember to begin your count with zero). That letter "a" tells us that the item being cataloged is a book. It is important to us because some automated systems will use a picture to represent the type of item being cataloged. We saw examples of this in chapter 4. If this space does not have the right code, then the record that the user sees will not be correct. Here are the proper codes for the materials you are most likely to be cataloging:

- a = book
- e = map
- g = movie, video, DVD, any moving picture viewed on a screen or computer
- i = non-musical sound recording; for example, audiobook either as tape cassette or CD
- j = musical sound recording in any format: tape cassette, CD, MP3 file, etc.
- m = computer file in any format: CD, web site, etc.

Variable Control Fields

Again, we have computer-coded information that makes little sense to us. Like-wise, there are no corresponding *AACR* rules for the information here. And, again, we are probably not very likely to make any changes to any of these tags.

001 14132483 The 001 field is called the Control Number. Your computer system will assign this number, and you need not worry about it.

005 20060824092851.0 The 005 field is called the Time and Date of Latest Trans-action field. The information is presented as year, month, day, and time. Here we see that this record was last modified on August 24, 2006 (20060824) at 9:25:51pm (092851.0). Again, this information is created by the computer and we will never change it.

008 051005s2006____ctu_b_001_0_eng The 008 field is called the Fixed Length Data Elements Field, and it is a little different from the 001 and 005 fields because we may in fact want to play with this one a little bit. The first six spaces in this tag (051005) are again created by the computer, so we'll leave that part alone.

The next five elements (s2006) are the type of publication date and the date of publication. Most of the time you will have an "s" in that number six space (again, we start counting from zero), which means there is a single date of publication and that is followed by the year of publication. This information comes from the 260 field. If you have a record where this information is blank, you now know how to easily enter in the right information.

The next spot is almost always blank unless there are more dates to deal with as in a magazine that has a beginning and ending date of publication. The next spaces (15–17) are important to us in that we can easily fix wrong information even though it really doesn't mean anything to the record. If this information is wrong, it can't hurt the way the record is filed by the computer or retrieved by the user. In this example we see the information as "ctu," which means that this book was published in Connecticut in the United States. If we look down at the 260 field we can see that this informa-tion is correct. In older records we might see "xxu," which means that the computer is not really sure where the item was published but is pretty sure it was published in the United States. To fix this part of the field, for U.S. publications only, we use the two letter postal code for the state and add a "u" to it. For example, a book published in Wisconsin would be coded as "wiu," or a computer program published in Texas would be coded "txu." Notice that the letters are lower case. By far the most common code is "nyu," which means the item was published in New York. The full list of codes for all countries can be found at the Library of Congress MARC 21 web site: http://www.loc.gov/marc/countries/countries_code.html.

The rest of the codes in this field change in meaning according the type of item being cataloged. Again, one can look at the MARC21 page for a full list of meanings for this part of the tag. The one element that is again the same for all types of items being cataloged is at the end of the tag. In our example the "eng" means that this item is in English. The thought was that one day, systems could be created that would search for the language of the item based on the information in the 008 tag. For small school and public library systems, this idea is still a dream, and so we mostly just leave this part of the tag alone. If you have a non-English language item and you want to change the code, see the LC MARC21 web site at: http://www.loc.gov/marc/languages/ for the list of language codes. It is quite all right to just accept whatever is in the field. However, if you are feeling brave, go ahead and play with this one.

VARIABLE LENGTH FIELDS

The following parts of the record make up the bulk of the MARC record. They are referred to as "variable length fields" because they can be long or short depending on the information contained in the field. Technically speaking there is no limit to the size of these fields, although some programs put a maximum length to them. In this area we will see some information that looks very familiar to us.

Variable Data Fields

The rest of the 0XX fields are a little bit easier for us to understand and to play with. These are the fields that deal with numbers that come from the item itself, such as ISBNs, or that we create, such as classification numbers.

010 __ $a 2005028602 This 010 field shows us the Library of Congress Control Number or the Library of Congress Catalog Card Number, sometimes referred to as the LCCN. This information can come from the item itself. The first part of the number refers to the date of publication; in this example, 2005. In the old days, the date was written as two digits with a hyphen as we see in this example: 94-27627. With the new millennium, the date changed to a four-digit number and the hyphen disappeared. Unless there is a typographical error, we will not be changing this number.

020 __ $a 1591580897 (pbk. : alk. paper) The 020 field is where one enters the International Standard Book Number, most commonly referred to as the ISBN. If you look in a book, you will see this number has hyphens in it, such as 1-59158-089-7. The ISBN is entered in the 020 field without the hyphens. In our example here, we have information in parentheses "(pbk : alk. paper)." This means that the book is paperback and on alkaline paper. Entering this information is optional. Again, unless there is an error in the number, we will not bother with this field.

040 __ $a DLC The 040 field shows the code of the library that has created and modified the catalog record. This is a code assigned by the Library of

Congress. Libraries may apply to get a library code by contacting LC (http://www.loc.gov/marc/organizations/#requests) and requesting a code.

$c DLC DLC is the abbreviation given to the Library of Congress.

$d DLC We will not alter this information at all. Subfields c and d note the institution that modified the record.

043 __ $a n-us—- The 043 field defines the place of action of the item. In this case, the story takes place in the United States. Again, the purpose of this field was to be able to search in this information, and as of now, for school and small public libraries, that search capability is still in the planning stages. If you are interested in making sure your records have this information, you can look at the country codes on the LC MARC21 web site: http://www.loc.gov/marc/geoareas/.

050 00 $a Z1037.A1 The 050 tag includes the Library of Congress Classification Number.

$b S237 2006

082 00 $a 028.5/50973 The 082 field includes the DDC number. The first indicator of zero (0) tells us that the unabridged DDC was used to create the number. If that first indicator had been a one (1) then we would know that the abridged edition was used. The second indicator zero (0) tells us that this number was created by the Library of Congress. If that second indicator was a four (4) then we would know someone else created the number. This field is often with a 092 (or sometimes 099) field which means that it is a local classification number.

$2 22 We see from the subfield 2 that the 22nd edition of the unabridged DDC was used to create the number.

MAIN ENTRY AND ADDED ENTRIES
(1XX AND 7XX FIELDS)

These fields help us to retrieve records based on the people who are responsible for the intellectual content of the item. They can be authors, illustrators, program designers, actors, producers, or anyone who is mentioned some place on the catalog record that you think your users will be looking for. The 1XX tag can only be used once in a record, but the 7XX tag can be used many times over. There are a variety of 1XX and 7XX fields. More often than not you will see only 100 or 700 fields that trace for people. But sometimes you may see a 110 or 710 tags that trace for the names of companies, called, in library terms, corporate bodies. For example, if Walt Disney Productions is responsible for the item you are cataloging, your users may well search for that company, and so to trace for that company you would need a 110 or 710 since it is a company and not a person. Part two of *AACR* (chapter 21) helps us to understand when to make a main or added entry. The examples below will show how the tags in this area work.

100 1_ $a Salem, Linda C. The information for the 100 tag is taken from the subfield c of the 245 field (see the example below). It is called the "main entry" tag but should be thought of as just one way to retrieve information about a person responsible for the content of the item. The information is entered with the last name first. Nothing is made up for this field. To check if you have all the information you need about this person, search the person's name in the LC authority catalog at the web site: http://authorities.loc.gov/. This tag may not be repeated.

110 2_ $a American Library Association. If the subfield c in the 245 field includes the name of a company who is responsible for the intellectual content of an item, then the 110 field is used for the main entry. More often than not, tracing for a company is listed in a 710 field rather than the 110 field. As with personal names, if you are not sure how to enter this information, check the LC authorities catalog. This tag may not be repeated.

700 1_ $a Williams, Garth. If the subfield c in the 245 field has more than one person, the first named person will be traced in the 100 tag and all others will be in traced in the 700 tag. Use one 700 tag for each person named; in other words do NOT do this:

700 1_ $a Williams, Garth and Sendak, Maurice.

Each person would have his own 700 tag, like this:

700 1_ $a Williams, Garth.
700 1_ $a Sendak, Maurice.

Like the 110 field, there is a 710 field for added tracings for companies. The difference between 1XX and 7XX fields is that where 1XX tag information can only come from the subfield c in the 245 field, the 7XX information can come from any place in the record. So if you want to trace for a narrator of an audiobook or a performer in a movie, you can do that even if the information is coming from elsewhere in the record; for example, if it is stated in a 5XX tag, you can trace it in a 7XX tag. There can also be a mix of 700 and 710 tags. For example, if you have a movie produced by Disney Home Video that stars Robin Williams and Tom Hanks, you would trace for those three in this way:

700 1_ $a Williams, Robin.
700 1_ $a Hanks, Tom.
710 2_ $a Walt Disney Home Video.

Notice the indicators in the examples. The first indicator, "1," for the 100 and 700 fields means the name is inverted order; Smith, John. Remember the problems with royalty. If you were making an entry for Princess Diana, the first indicator would be "0," meaning the first thing you see in the field is a first name, not a last name. In the 110 and 710 fields, the first indicator has a different meaning. The "2" in these two fields means that the name of the company is in "direct order"; that is, it is entered as it looks, not in any kind of inverted order. This field is repeatable.

Title, Other Title Information, Statement of Responsibility: AACR, 1.1B[1]

245 10 $a Children's literature studies In subfield a, the title proper, the first part of the title is entered; notice that the second indicator is zero because we can file this title under "c" for "children's."

:$b cases and discussions Subfield b is always preceded by a colon unless you have a translated title, in which case it is preceded by an equals sign (=); the information in this subfield is considered for a title tracing, but we probably would not do so for this particular title information because it is too generic; that is, it doesn't really mean anything special to this work.

/$c Linda C. Salem. Subfield c is always preceded by a slash (/) and always ends with a period (.). Salem will be traced in the main entry, 100 field.

Another Example

245 00 $a 21 days to Baghdad Notice the indicators here; "0" in the first spot to show that there is no 1XX tag; in films there is very seldom a named (1XX) main entry; and the second indicator is also "0," so the computer will file this under "2." See below for dealing with numbers in title.

$h [videorecording] Here is the information that this item is not a book

:$b the inside story of the military campaign to topple Saddam Hussein Again the subfield is preceded by the colon; see below for how we deal with this other title information.

/$c narrated by Terry MacDonald. Again, this subfield is preceded by a slash (/); even though MacDonald narrated this video, he doesn't get the main entry (100 field) because he is not responsible for the intellectual content of the item; he is simply the narrator. However, we do want to trace for him so we put him down in a 700 field.

246 3_ $a Twenty one days to Baghdad Note how we trace for the title as if the word had been written out. We do this for all titles where there is a number in the first five words of a title so the computer will retrieve the title whether the user types in a number or a word. The indicators in this field have a variety of meanings. In our example, we have provided two common indicators. The first indicator, "3," tells the computer that we want it to trace for this title but there is no need to make a note about it in the catalog record. This is usually what we want to do. The second indicator is a little bit different. It tells the computer what kind of other title information we have. It is a picky detail and may in short term mean nothing to us or our computer systems. But we need to know that if the second indicator is blank as it is in our example here, then we are defining what kind of other title information this is. This works best when we're changing the numeral (in this case 21) to the written word ("twenty one").

246 3_ $a Twentyone days to Baghdad Here we have repeated the number word as one word instead of two as we did above. We do this in an attempt to cover the options the user may take. Is the word "twenty one," "twenty-one," or "twentyone"? My spell check on my computer tells me the number 21 can be written as two words or hyphenated but that it is not one word. What happens to the user who does type in the number as one word or the cataloger who makes a mistake and enters the record as one word? In working with numbers we try to cover all bases. Likewise, "mistakes" in titles, such as *The Worst Best School Year Ever* that we discussed in chapter 3, can be dealt with using the 246 field to correct mistakes. In this case we might have one 246 field for The worst school year ever and another for The best school year ever.

246 30 $a Inside story of the military campaign to topple Saddam Hussein Here we enter the second part of the title as shown in subfield b of the 245 field. Remember that in the 245 field the second indicator tells the computer to skip the initial article. In the 246 field we don't have an indicator to tell the computer to do this. The result is that we have to drop the initial article (as we have done in this example) and start with the first word that is not an article. We make this other title information tracing when the information in the subfield b of the 245 tag is substantial. That means that if the subtitle is something generic, like "a love story" or "the true story" or something similar, the user is not likely to search and could apply to a number of different items; then we do not fill in a 246 field for that item. Notice in this example we have a new value for the second indicator: "0." This means that we are providing a "portion" of the title. A title portion is usually information in subfield b in the 245 field, although at times it can come from the subfield a in the 245 field.

700 1_ $a MacDonald, Terry. This is how we trace for other authors or creators in the subfield c of the 245 field and also how we trace for people noted in the 5XX tags as we see fit. In this case we have the narrator of the work. We can also have second authors, illustrators, directors, actors, etc. Any person's name we think our users might be looking for we put in the 700 field. Remember that the 700 field may be repeated, so if there are two names we want to trace for, then we will add two 700 fields.

Edition Information: AACR 1.2

250 __ $a 2nd ed.

250 __ $a 20th anniversary ed.

250 __ $a Version 4.5. In these three examples we have the edition statements. If there is something on the item that refers to an edition, version, or special issue, that information is recorded here in the 250 field. Notice that "edition" is abbreviated to "ed," but "version" is not abbreviated.

Publication Information: AACR 1.4

260 __ $a Westport, Conn. Record here the place of publication as written on the item except that states can be abbreviated.

> **:$b Libraries Unlimited** Record here the name of the publisher. This subfield is preceded by a colon.

> **,c$2006.** Record here the date of publication. If there is a copyright date instead of a publication date it is recorded like this: cc2006. Do not confuse the name of the subfield "c" for the copyright abbreviation "c." Use "p" for sound recordings if that's what you see on the item. Printing dates are not the same as publication and copyright dates; do not use printing dates in the subfield c.

Physical Description: AACR 1.5

300 __ $a xi, 153 p. Record here the "extent of the item"; in other words, the number of pages of a book, or the number of discs in a sound or movie recording. If the book's pages have roman numerals that are separate from the Arabic numbers (page numbers start over with "1"), add the Roman numerals if there are 10 (x) or more. Children's books with unnumbered pages are recorded as: 1 v. (unpaged), although in old catalog records you may well see the numbers in brackets : [32 p.], which means the cataloger counted the pages. For adult books you must count the pages and enter the information in brackets, but for children's books you do not need to count the pages. For non-book materials, add the running time. For example:

> 300 __ $a 14 sound discs (ca. 9 hrs.)

> **:$b ill.** If your book has pictures, use the abbreviation "ill." to note this, although with older cataloging you may see more information such as: maps, port., etc. For non-book items, enter here the type of recording such as sound (sd.) or color of images (col. or b&w). For example:

> : $b sd., col.

> **; $c26 cm.** Measure the height of the book in centimeters. For non-book items, use standard measure of CDs (4 3/4 in.), tapes (1/2 in.), etc. Cassette tapes are assumed to be the standard size (approximately 3" x 2") and so there is no subfield c for cassette tapes that are standard size. If the cassette tape you have is not a standard size, record the measurement of height x length in inches.

+$e 1 puppet. Add a subfield e if there is other material with your item that is important to record. Describe the accompanying material in parentheses if necessary. For example, a book with a tape cassette:

300 __ $a 1 sound cassette (ca. 30 min.)
:$b digital
+$e 1 book (28 p. : ill ; 24 cm)

If you do not describe the item in parentheses, this field ends in a period (.), but if you add a description within parentheses then there is no period at the end of this field.

Series Title Information: AACR 1.6

440 _0 $a Choose your own adventure The title of the series (if there is one) is recorded in this field. Notice that the first indicator is blank but the second indicator is not. The second indicator here works the same way that the second indicator in the 245 field works; it tells the computer to skip the initial articles (the, a, an). Our series title in this example does not begin with an initial article, so we're all right with "0" value. This field does not end with a period (.).

$v #1 If your item has a volume number attached to it, record that here in the subfield v. Notice in our example that the number "1" is preceded by the number sign (#). That is because it is noted as "#1" on the item. If our item was noted as "Number 1" then we would record it as: v no.1. If our item was noted as "Volume 1" then we would record that as: v vol.1.

Notes Area: AACR 1.7

Before we show example notes fields, remember that there is lots of information that can go into the notes area. See the LC MARC manual for a full list of fields for this area: http://www.loc.gov/marc/bibliographic/bd5xx.html. The following fields are just examples of the information that is recorded in this part of the catalog record. In looking at cataloging, you may see some or none of these fields; it depends on the detail demanded of the cataloger in creating the record. All of these tags are repeatable and they all end in a period (.).

500 __ $a Title taken from home page screen. If you have a non-book item, you must define the source of the title. In this example, we have a web site, and the title is taken from the home page. Some web sites have multiple parts that can in fact stand on their own. Defining the source of the title helps the user know if this is a main web page or a part of a web page.

500 __ $a Includes index. This piece of information tells us that the book has an index. Some people might argue that it is silly to include so much detail about a book, but making a note that the item has an index can be very helpful for someone looking for some specific piece of information without having to read the entire book.

500 __ $a VHS. If you have a videotape, you must define the type of tape it is. These days we are hard pressed to find a video that is not in VHS format, but when this note was standardized there were a couple of different types of videotape formats. Perhaps one day we will no longer need to have this note.

504 __ $a Includes bibliographical references and index. If a book has both a bibliography and an index, then that note is recorded in the 504 field. As we saw above, if there is only an index, then that is recorded in the 500 field. If it has only a bibliography (or any kind of list, a list of recordings, called a discography, or web sites, called a webliography), then that is recorded here in the 504 field.

505 0_ $a They way we were — The way we want to be — The way we will be. This is the note area for the table of contents. There are several ways to note a table of contents and reasons for doing so. You may have a multiple volume set with each book having a different title; or you may have a collection of short stories and you want to note specific stories you know your readers will be looking for or to list the entire table of contents.

508 __ $a Producer, Ken Burns; director, Kathy Donahue; musical score, John Williams. This field is used to make note of the creators of an item, usually a film, software program, or any item where you are not sure who is the chief person responsible and so you need to make note of many people; typically this is used only for non-book items.

511 0_ $a Narrator, Peter Ustinov; voices of Tom Hanks, Robin Williams, Sally Field. This field is used to note the performers on a non-book item such as the members of a rock group or the actors in a film or the performers in a dance movie.

520 __ $a Two kids run away from their parents only to find that there is no place like home. This is by far the most used 5XX field of the bunch. This is the place for a summary of the item. It is a crucial note for a work of fiction and extremely helpful for a work of non-fiction regardless of the format of the item.

521 __ $a Rated G for general audiences. The 521 field is used to note the audience focus for the item. In this example, we have the MAPP rating. The type of audience note is defined by the first indicator: 0 for reading grade level, 1 for reading interest age level, and 2 for reading interest grade level. Often all you will see in the MARC record is the field, the indicator, and a number. The information is then translated by the computer system and displayed in English for the user. Here are some other examples:

521 0_ $a 5–7. [reading level for grades 5–7; usually notes some scientific way of determining the difficulty of the words and sentence structure to come up with an appropriate grade level audience]

521 1_ $a 4–6. [kids ages 4–6 will probably like this]

521 2_ $a 5. [kids in grade 5 will probably like this]

538 __ $a System Requirements: This note is used to list the technical requirements needed for playback. It can be as simple as noting the need for a DVD player to as complicated as describing the exact program and computer needs. Usually this information is taken directly from the box in which the item is housed.

546 __ $a Translated from the Russian. This note is used to describe anything about the language of the item; if it is a translation or if it has bilingual text as shown in the next example:

> 546 __ $a Includes English subtitles.

586 __ $a Caldecott Honor Book, 1999. If your item won any kind of award, that information is recorded in this field. There is no standard way of making this note, so you will write it out in a way that makes the most sense to your users. Here is another example of this note field:

> 586 __ $a Academy Award for best actor, 1998.

Subject Area

This is not part of the physical description of the item so it is not covered under *AACR*. This is where *LCSH*, *Sears*, and other subject heading vocabularies come into play. All of these fields are repeatable, and they all end with a period (.). The headings listed below were all retrieved from the Library of Congress catalog (http://catalog.loc.gov/) by using the subject search link and looking at the MARC records.

600 10 $aChurchill, Winston

> **,$cSir**
> **,$d1874–1965**
> **$xChildhood and youth.** This item is about the British Prime Minister Sir Winston Churchill when he was growing up.

600 11 $a Einstein, Albert

> **,$d 1879–1965.** This is a LC/AC heading, we know this by the "1" in the second indicator spot.

610 20 $a World Trade Center (New York, N.Y.)
610 21 $a World Trade Center (New York, N.Y.) Note here that both the LC and the LC/AC are the same. The heading for this corporate heading has been established for both adults and children. That happens sometimes that they are exactly the same.

650 _0 $a Aerialists

$z France
$v Juvenile literature.

650 _1 $aAerialists. Note here the differences between the LC and the LC/AC headings. The LC heading offers us much more detail, but it also gives us the subdivision "Juvenile literature," which some kids may be unhappy with (no one wants to be a "juvenile") and so the LC/AC heading which by definition tends to offer less detail but also gets rid of that juvenile notation. We know that the two headings are different from the indicators, but our users in the catalog will probably wonder why there are two very similar headings in the record. For your library, you may decide to just delete the LC headings for kids' books to avoid confusion, but be careful as you don't want to delete headings that are different enough to offer the user more access points.

651 _0 $a Grand Canyon (Ariz.)
651 _7 $a Grand Canyon (Ariz.)

$2sears Here we see two subject headings for a geographic location. Although they are both the same, the first one is from LC. We know this because the second indicator is 0. The second subject heading is from the Sears list. We know this because the second indicator 7 tells us that some list besides LC is being used and the subfield 2 tells us that the list being used is Sears. Note that "sears" is not capitalized in the subfield 2.

This concludes our annotated look at a MARC record. See Appendix D for a MARC template.

NOTE

1.   The *Anglo-American Cataloging Rules* are divided into two parts. In part one, chapter 1 presents the general rules and chapters 2–13 apply those rules for specific formats: books, movies, maps, etc. In this appendix, the general rules from chapter 1 only will be cited. Unfortunately there is no free resource to look at for the *AACR* standards. Gorman's *Concise Guide to AACR* (see resources list) is organized around the rule numbers. It would make this book unnecessarily long to include the full description of each rule. I am supplying the rule numbers for two reasons; first, so that we all remember that the MARC format is simply a tool to translate information from the item to the computer using standardized cataloging rules; and second, so that if you have the desire to do so, you can easily look up the rules that are being addressed for each field.

APPENDIX D

MARC Record Template

This template is almost a complete duplicate of Appendix C but without all of the explanations; just the tags with example information. The information you put in each tag will depend on your item in hand. Remember that these are just the more common tags; this is not a complete list of all available tags. To see all of the tags, go to the LC MARC21 web page: http://www.loc.gov/marc/bibliographic/ecbdhome.html.

Leader: 01361cam_a2200301_a_450_

001 14132483

005 20060824092851.0

008 051005s2006____ctu_b_001_0_eng

010 __ $a 2005028602

020 __ $a 1591580897 (pbk. : alk. paper)

040 __ $a DLC

      $c DLC

      $d DLC

043 __ $a n-us---

050 00 $a Z1037.A1

      $b S237 2006

082 00 $a 028.5/50973

      $2 22

100 1_ $a Salem, Linda C.

245 00 $a 21 days to Baghdad

      $h [videorecording]

      :$b the inside story of the military campaign to topple Saddam Hussein

      /$c narrated by Terry MacDonald.

246 3_ $a Twenty one days to Baghdad

246 3_ $a Twentyone days to Baghdad

246 30 $a Inside story of the military campaign to topple Saddam Hussein

250 __ $a 20th anniversary ed.

260 __ $a Westport, Conn.

      :$b Libraries Unlimited

      ,c$2006.

300 __ a 14 sound discs (ca. 9 hrs.)

       :$b digital

       ;$c 4 3/4 in.

       +$e 1 puppet.

440 _0 $a Choose your own adventure

       $v #1

500 __ $a Title taken from home page screen.

500 __ $a Includes index.

500 __ $a CD.

504 __ $a Includes bibliographical references and index.

505 0_ $a They way we were -- The way we want to be -- The way we will be.

508 __ $a Producer, Ken Burns ; director, Kathy Donahue ; musical score, John
            Williams.

511 0_ $a Narrator, Peter Ustinov ; voices of Tom Hanks, Robin Williams, Sally
            Field.

520 __ $a Two kids run away from their parents only to find that there is no place
            like home.

521 __ $a Rated G for general audiences.

521 0_ $a 5-7.

521 1_ $a 4-6.

521 2_ $a 5.

538 __ $a System Requirements: CD or DVD player.

546 __ $a Translated from the Russian.

586 __ $a Caldecott Honor Book, 1999.

600 10 $aChurchill, Winston

,$cSir

,$d1874-1965

$xChildhood and youth.

600 11 $a Einstein, Albert

,$d 1879-1965.

610 20 $a World Trade Center (New York, N.Y.)

610 21 $a World Trade Center (New York, N.Y.)

650 _0 $a Aerialists

$z France

$v Juvenile literature.

650 _1 $aAerialists.

651 _0 $a Grand Canyon (Ariz.)

700 1_ $a Williams, Garth.

700 1_ $a MacDonald, Terry.

INDEX

ABOUT THE AUTHOR

ALLISON G. KAPLAN is associate faculty associate in the School of Library and Information Studies, University of Wisconsin–Madison.

Made in the USA
Las Vegas, NV
15 June 2021